MW00784057

The Collected Poetry of William Cowper

Volume I

William Cowper was born 26th November 1731 in Berkhamsted, Hertfordshire. Traumatically he and his brother, John, were the only survivors, out of seven, to survive infancy. His mother died when he was six.

His education, after several temporary schools, was stabilised at Westminster school. Here he established several life-long friendships and a dedication to Latin. Upon leaving he was articled to a solicitor in London and spent almost a decade training in Law. In 1763 he was offered a Clerkship of Journals in the House of Lords. With the examinations approaching Cowper had a mental breakdown. He tried to commit suicide three times and a period of depression and insanity seemed to settle on him. The end of this unhappy period saw him find refuge in fervent evangelical Christianity, and it was also the inspiration behind his much-loved hymns.

This led to a collaboration with John Newton in writing 'Olney Hymns'.

However dark forces were about to overwhelm Cowper. In 1773, he experienced a devastating attack of insanity, believing that he was eternally condemned to hell, and that God was instructing him to make a sacrifice of his own life. With great care and devotion his friend, Mary Unwin, nursed him back to health.

In 1781 Cowper had the good fortune to meet a widow, Lady Austen, who inspired a new bout of poetry writing. Cowper himself tells of the genesis of what some have considered his most substantial work, 'The Task'.

In 1786 he began his translations from the Greek into blank verse of Homer's 'The Iliad' and 'The Odyssey'. These translations, published in 1791, were the most significant since those of Alexander Pope earlier in the century.

Mary Unwin died in 1796, plunging Cowper into a gloom from which he never fully recovered though he did continue to write.

William Cowper was seized with dropsy and died on 25th April 1800.

Index of Contents

PREFACE TO THE POEMS

When an author, by appearing in print, requests an audience of the public, and is upon the point of speaking for himself, whoever presumes to step before him with a preface, and to say, "Nay, but hear me first," should have something worthy of attention to offer, or he will be justly deemed officious and impertinent. The judicious reader has probably, upon other occasions, been beforehand with me in this reflection: and I am not very willing it should now be applied to me, however I may seem to expose myself to the danger of it. But the thought of having my own name perpetuated in connexion with the name in the title-page is so pleasing and flattering to the feelings of my heart, that I am content to risk something for the gratification.

This Preface is not designed to commend the Poems to which it is prefixed. My testimony would be insufficient for those who are not qualified to judge properly for themselves, and unnecessary to those who are. Besides, the reasons which render it improper and unseemly for a man to celebrate his own performances, or those of his nearest relatives, will have some influence in suppressing much of what he might otherwise wish to say in favour of a friend, when that friend is indeed an alter idem, and excites almost the same emotions of sensibility and affection as he feels for himself.

It is very probable these Poems may come into the hands of some persons, in whom the sight of the author's name will awaken a recollection of incidents and scenes, which through length of time they had almost forgotten. They will be reminded of one, who was once the companion of their chosen hours, and who set out with them in early life in the paths which lead to literary honours, to influence and affluence, with equal prospects of success. But he was suddenly and powerfully withdrawn from those pursuits, and he left them without regret; yet not till he had sufficient opportunity of counting the cost, and of knowing the value of what he gave up. If happiness could have been found in classical attainments, in an elegant taste, in the exertions of wit, fancy, and genius, and in the esteem and converse of such persons, as in these respects were most congenial with himself, he would have been happy. But he was not—he wondered (as thousands in a similar situation still do) that he should continue dissatisfied, with all the means apparently conducive to satisfaction within his reach—But in due time the cause of his disappointment was discovered to him—he had lived without God in the world. In a memorable hour, the wisdom which is from above visited his heart. Then he felt himself a wanderer, and then he found a guide. Upon this change of views, a change of plan and conduct followed of course. When he saw the busy and the gay world in its true light, he left it with as little reluctance as a prisoner, when called to liberty, leaves his dungeon. Not that he became a Cynic or an Ascetic—a heart filled with love to God will assuredly breathe benevolence to men. But the turn of his temper inclining him to rural life, he indulged it, and, the providence of God evidently preparing his way and marking out his retreat, he retired into the country. By these steps the good hand of God, unknown to me, was providing for me one of the principal blessings of my life; a friend and a counsellor, in whose company for almost seven years, though we were seldom seven successive waking hours separated, I always found new pleasure—a friend who was not only a comfort to myself, but a blessing to the affectionate poor people among whom I then lived.

Some time after inclination had thus removed him from the hurry and bustle of life, he was still more secluded by a long indisposition, and my pleasure was succeeded by a proportionable degree of anxiety and concern. But a hope, that the God whom he served would support him under his affliction, and at length vouchsafe him a happy deliverance, never forsook me. The desirable crisis, I trust, is now nearly approaching. The dawn, the presage of returning day, is already arrived. He is again enabled to resume his pen, and some of the first fruits of his recovery are here presented to the public. In his principal subjects, the same acumen, which distinguished him in the early period of life, is happily employed in illustrating and enforcing the truths of which he received such deep and unalterable impressions in his maturer years. His satire, if it may be called so, is benevolent, (like the operations of the skilful and humane surgeon, who wounds only to heal,) dictated by a just regard for the honour of God, an indignant grief excited by the profligacy of the age, and a tender compassion for the souls of men.

His favourite topics are least insisted on in the piece entitled Table Talk; which therefore, with some regard to the prevailing taste, and that those, who are governed by it, may not be discouraged at the very threshold from proceeding farther, is placed first. In most of the large poems which follow, his leading design is more explicitly avowed and pursued. He aims to communicate his own perceptions of the truth, beauty, and influence of the religion of the Bible—a religion, which, however discredited by the misconduct of many, who have not renounced the Christian name, proves itself, when rightly understood, and cordially embraced, to be the grand desideratum, which alone can relieve the mind of man from painful and unavoidable anxieties, inspire it with stable peace and solid hope, and furnish those motives and prospects which, in the present state of things, are absolutely necessary to produce a conduct worthy of a rational creature, distinguished by a vastness of capacity which no assemblage of earthly good can satisfy, and by a principle and pre-intimation of immortality.

At a time when hypothesis and conjecture in philosophy are so justly exploded, and little is considered as deserving the name of knowledge, which will not stand the test of experiment, the very use of the term experimental in religious concernments is by too many unhappily rejected with disgust. But we well know, that they, who affect to despise the inward feelings which religious persons speak of, and to treat them as enthusiasm and folly, have inward feelings of their own, which, though they would, they cannot, suppress. We have been too long in the secret ourselves, to account the proud, the ambitious, or the voluptuous, happy. We must lose the remembrance of what we once were, before we can believe that a man is satisfied with himself, merely because he endeavours to appear so. A smile upon the face is often but a mask worn occasionally and in company, to prevent, if possible, a suspicion of what at the same time is passing in the heart. We know that there are people who seldom smile when they are alone, who therefore are glad to hide themselves in a throng from the violence of their own reflections; and who, while by their looks and their language they wish to persuade us they are happy, would be glad to change their conditions with a dog. But in defiance of all their efforts they continue to think, forbode, and tremble. This we know, for it has been our own state, and therefore we know how to commiserate it in others.—From this state the Bible relieved us—when we were led to read it with attention, we found ourselves described. We learned the causes of our inquietude—we were directed to a method of relief—we tried, and we were not disappointed.

Deus nobis hæc otia fecit.

We are now certain that the gospel of Christ is the power of God unto salvation to every one that believeth. It has reconciled us to God, and to ourselves, to our duty and our situation. It is the balm and cordial of the present life, and a sovereign antidote against the fear of death.

Sed hactenus hæc. Some smaller pieces upon less important subjects close the volume. Not one of them, I believe, was written with a view to publication, but I was unwilling they should be omitted.

John Newton.

Charles Square, Hoxton,
February 18, 1782.

TABLE TALK

Si te fortè meæ gravis uret sarcina chartæ,
Abjicito.
HOR. LIB. I. EP. 13.

THE ARGUMENT

True and false glory—Kings made for man—Attributes of royalty in England—Quevedo's satire on kings—Kings objects of pity—Inquiry concerning the cause of Englishmen's scorn of arbitrary rule—Character of the Englishman and the Frenchman—Charms of freedom—Freedom sometimes needs the restraint of discipline—Reference to the riots in London—Tribute to Lord Chatham—Political state of England—The vices that debase her portend her downfall—Political events the instruments of Providence—The poet disclaims prophetic inspiration—The choice of a mean subject denotes a weak mind—Reference to Homer, Virgil, and Milton—Progress of poesy—The poet laments that religion is not more frequently united with poetry.

A. You told me, I remember, glory, built
On selfish principles, is shame and guilt:
The deeds, that men admire as half divine,
Stark naught, because corrupt in their design.
Strange doctrine this! that without scruple tears
The laurel that the very lightning spares;
Brings down the warrior's trophy to the dust,
And eats into his bloody sword like rust.

B. I grant that, men continuing what they are,
Fierce, avaricious, proud, there must be war,
And never meant the rule should be applied
To him that fights with justice on his side.
  Let laurels drench'd in pure Parnassian dews
Reward his memory, dear to every muse,
Who, with a courage of unshaken root,
In honour's field advancing his firm foot,
Plants it upon the line that Justice draws,
And will prevail or perish in her cause.

'Tis to the virtues of such men man owes
His portion in the good that Heaven bestows.
And, when recording History displays
Feats of renown, though wrought in ancient days,
Tells of a few stout hearts, that fought and died,
Where duty placed them, at their country's side;
The man that is not moved with what he reads,
That takes not fire at their heroic deeds,
Unworthy of the blessings of the brave,
Is base in kind, and born to be a slave.
  But let eternal infamy pursue
The wretch to nought but his ambition true,
Who, for the sake of filling with one blast
The post-horns of all Europe, lays her waste.
Think yourself stationed on a towering rock,
To see a people scattered like a flock,
Some royal mastiff panting at their heels,
With all the savage thirst a tiger feels;
Then view him self-proclaim'd in a gazette
Chief monster that has plagued the nations yet.
The globe and sceptre in such hands misplaced,
Those ensigns of dominion, how disgraced!
The glass, that bids man mark the fleeting hour,
And Death's own scythe, would better speak his power;
Then grace the bony phantom in their stead
With the king's shoulder-knot and gay cockade;
Clothe the twin brethren in each other's dress,
The same their occupation and success.

A. 'Tis your belief the world was made for man;
Kings do but reason on the self-same plan:
Maintaining yours, you cannot theirs condemn,
Who think, or seem to think, man made for them.

B. Seldom, alas! the power of logic reigns
With much sufficiency in royal brains;
Such reasoning falls like an inverted cone,
Wanting its proper base to stand upon.
Man made for kings! those optics are but dim
That tell you so—say, rather, they for him.
That were indeed a king-ennobling thought,
Could they, or would they, reason as they ought.
The diadem, with mighty projects lined,
To catch renown by ruining mankind,
Is worth, with all its gold and glittering store,
Just what the toy will sell for, and no more.
  Oh! bright occasions of dispensing good,
How seldom used, how little understood!

To pour in Virtue's lap her just reward;
Keep Vice restrain'd behind a double guard;
To quell the faction that affronts the throne
By silent magnanimity alone;
To nurse with tender care the thriving arts;
Watch every beam Philosophy imparts;
To give religion her unbridled scope,
Nor judge by statute a believer's hope;
With close fidelity and love unfeign'd
To keep the matrimonial bond unstain'd;
Covetous only of a virtuous praise;
His life a lesson to the land he sways;
To touch the sword with conscientious awe,
Nor draw it but when duty bids him draw;
To sheath it in the peace-restoring close
With joy beyond what victory bestows—
Blest country, where these kingly glories shine!
Blest England, if this happiness be thine!

A. Guard what you say: the patriotic tribe
Will sneer, and charge you with a bribe.—B. A bribe?
The worth of his three kingdoms I defy,
To lure me to the baseness of a lie;
And, of all lies, (be that one poet's boast,)
The lie that flatters I abhor the most.
Those arts be theirs who hate his gentle reign,
But he that loves him has no need to feign.

A. Your smooth eulogium, to one crown address'd,
Seems to imply a censure on the rest.

B. Quevedo, as he tells his sober tale,
Ask'd, when in hell, to see the royal jail;
Approv'd their method in all other things;
But where, good sir, do you confine your kings?
There—said his guide—the group is in full view.
Indeed!—replied the don—there are but few.
His black interpreter the charge disdain'd—
Few, fellow?—there are all that ever reign'd.
Wit, undistinguishing, is apt to strike
The guilty and not guilty both alike:
I grant the sarcasm is too severe,
And we can readily refute it here;
While Alfred's name, the father of his age,
And the Sixth Edward's grace the historic page.

A. Kings then at last have but the lot of all:
By their own conduct they must stand or fall.

B. True. While they live, the courtly laureate pays
His quitrent ode, his peppercorn of praise,
And many a dunce, whose fingers itch to write,
Adds, as he can, his tributary mite:
A subject's faults a subject may proclaim,
A monarch's errors are forbidden game!
Thus, free from censure, overawed by fear,
And prais'd for virtues that they scorn to wear,
The fleeting forms of majesty engage
Respect, while stalking o'er life's narrow stage:
Then leave their crimes for history to scan,
And ask, with busy scorn, Was this the man?
  I pity kings, whom worship waits upon,
Obsequious from the cradle to the throne;
Before whose infant eyes the flatterer bows,
And binds a wreath about their baby brows:
Whom education stiffens into state,
And death awakens from that dream too late.
Oh! if servility with supple knees,
Whose trade it is to smile, to crouch, to please;
If smooth dissimulation, skill'd to grace
A devil's purpose with an angel's face;
If smiling peeresses and simpering peers,
Encompassing his throne a few short years;
If the gilt carriage and the pamper'd steed,
That wants no driving, and disdains the lead:
If guards, mechanically form'd in ranks,
Playing, at beat of drum, their martial pranks,
Shouldering and standing as if stuck to stone,
While condescending majesty looks on—
If monarchy consist in such base things,
Sighing, I say again, I pity kings!
  To be suspected, thwarted, and withstood,
E'en when he labours for his country's good;
To see a band call'd patriot for no cause,
But that they catch at popular applause,
Careless of all the anxiety he feels,
Hook disappointment on the public wheels;
With all their flippant fluency of tongue,
Most confident, when palpably most wrong—
If this be kingly, then farewell for me
All kingship, and may I be poor and free!
  To be the Table Talk of clubs up stairs,
To which the unwash'd artificer repairs,
To indulge his genius after long fatigue,
By diving into cabinet intrigue;
(For what kings deem a toil, as well they may,

To him is relaxation, and mere play:)
To win no praise when well wrought plans prevail,
But to be rudely censur'd when they fail;
To doubt the love his favourites may pretend,
And in reality to find no friend;
If he indulge a cultivated taste,
His galleries with the works of art well graced,
To hear it call'd extravagance and waste;
If these attendants, and if such as these,
Must follow royalty, then welcome ease;
However humble and confined the sphere,
Happy the state that has not these to fear!

A. Thus men, whose thoughts contemplative have dwelt
On situations that they never felt,
Start up sagacious, cover'd with the dust
Of dreaming study and pedantic rust,
And prate and preach about what others prove,
As if the world and they were hand and glove.
Leave kingly backs to cope with kingly cares;
They have their weight to carry, subjects theirs;
Poets, of all men, ever least regret
Increasing taxes and the nation's debt.
Could you contrive the payment, and rehearse
The mighty plan, oracular, in verse,
No bard, howe'er majestic, old or new,
Should claim my fix'd attention more than you.

B. Not Brindley nor Bridgewater would essay
To turn the course of Helicon that way:
Nor would the Nine consent the sacred tide
Should purl amidst the traffic of Cheapside,
Or tinkle in 'Change Alley, to amuse
The leathern ears of stockjobbers and Jews.

A. Vouchsafe, at least, to pitch the key of rhyme,
To themes more pertinent, if less sublime.
When ministers and ministerial arts;
Patriots, who love good places at their hearts;
When admirals, extoll'd for standing still,
Or doing nothing with a deal of skill;
Generals, who will not conquer when they may,
Firm friends to peace, to pleasure, and good pay;
When Freedom, wounded almost to despair,
Though discontent alone can find out where—
When themes like these employ the poet's tongue,
I hear as mute as if a syren sung.
Or tell me, if you can, what power maintains

A Briton's scorn of arbitrary chains?
That were a theme might animate the dead,
And move the lips of poets cast in lead.

B. The cause, though worth the search, may yet elude
Conjecture and remark, however shrewd.
They take, perhaps, a well directed aim,
Who seek it in his climate and his frame.
Liberal in all things else, yet Nature here
With stern severity deals out the year.
Winter invades the spring, and often pours
A chilling flood on summer's drooping flowers;
Unwelcome vapours quench autumnal beams,
Ungenial blasts attending curl the streams:
The peasants urge their harvest, ply the fork
With double toil, and shiver at their work;
Thus with a rigour, for his good design'd,
She rears her favourite man of all mankind,
His form robust, and of elastic tone,
Proportion'd well, half muscle and half bone,
Supplies with warm activity and force
A mind well lodged, and masculine of course.
Hence Liberty, sweet Liberty inspires
And keeps alive his fierce but noble fires.
Patient of constitutional control,
He bears it with meek manliness of soul;
But, if authority grow wanton, woe
To him that treads upon his free-born toe;
One step beyond the boundary of the laws
Fires him at once in Freedom's glorious cause.
Thus proud Prerogative, not much rever'd,
Is seldom felt, though sometimes seen and heard;
And in his cage, like parrot fine and gay,
Is kept to strut, look big, and talk away.
   Born in a climate softer far than ours,
Not form'd like us, with such Herculean powers,
The Frenchman, easy, debonair, and brisk,
Give him his lass, his fiddle, and his frisk,
Is always happy, reign whoever may,
And laughs the sense of misery far away:
He drinks his simple beverage with a gust;
And, feasting on an onion and a crust,
We never feel the alacrity and joy
With which he shouts and carols, Vive le Roi!
Filled with as much true merriment and glee
As if he heard his king say—Slave, be free.
   Thus happiness depends, as Nature shows,
Less on exterior things than most suppose.

Vigilant over all that he has made,
Kind Providence attends with gracious aid;
Bids equity throughout his works prevail,
And weighs the nations in an even scale;
He can encourage slavery to a smile,
And fill with discontent a British isle.

A. Freeman and slave then, if the case be such,
Stand on a level; and you prove too much:
If all men indiscriminately share
His fostering power, and tutelary care,
As well be yoked by Despotism's hand,
As dwell at large in Britain's charter'd land.

B. No. Freedom has a thousand charms to show,
That slaves, howe'er contented, never know.
The mind attains beneath her happy reign
The growth that Nature meant she should attain;
The varied fields of science, ever new,
Opening and wider opening on her view,
She ventures onward with a prosperous force,
While no base fear impedes her in her course:
Religion, richest favour of the skies,
Stands most reveal'd before the freeman's eyes;
No shades of superstition blot the day,
Liberty chases all that gloom away.
The soul, emancipated, unoppress'd,
Free to prove all things and hold fast the best,
Learns much; and to a thousand listening minds
Communicates with joy the good she finds;
Courage in arms, and ever prompt to show
His manly forehead to the fiercest foe;
Glorious in war, but for the sake of peace,
His spirits rising as his toils increase,
Guards well what arts and industry have won,
And Freedom claims him for her firstborn son.
Slaves fight for what were better cast away—
The chain that binds them, and a tyrant's sway,
But they that fight for freedom undertake
The noblest cause mankind can have at stake:
Religion, virtue, truth, whate'er we call
A blessing—freedom is the pledge of all.
O Liberty! the prisoner's pleasing dream,
The poet's muse, his passion, and his theme;
Genius is thine, and thou art Fancy's nurse;
Lost without thee the ennobling powers of verse;
Heroic song from thy free touch acquires
Its clearest tone, the rapture it inspires.

Place me where Winter breathes his keenest air,
And I will sing, if Liberty be there;
And I will sing at Liberty's dear feet,
In Afric's torrid clime, or India's fiercest heat.

A. Sing where you please; in such a cause I grant
An English poet's privilege to rant;
But is not Freedom—at least, is not ours
Too apt to play the wanton with her powers,
Grow freakish, and, o'erleaping every mound,
Spread anarchy and terror all around?

B. Agreed. But would you sell or slay your horse
For bounding and curveting in his course?
Or if, when ridden with a careless rein,
He break away, and seek the distant plain?
No. His high mettle, under good control,
Gives him Olympic speed, and shoots him to the goal.
  Let Discipline employ her wholesome arts;
Let magistrates alert perform their parts,
Not skulk or put on a prudential mask,
As if their duty were a desperate task;
Let active laws apply the needful curb,
To guard the peace that riot would disturb;
And Liberty, preserved from wild excess,
Shall raise no feuds for armies to suppress.
When Tumult lately burst his prison door,
And set plebeian thousands in a roar;
When he usurp'd authority's just place,
And dared to look his master in the face;
When the rude rabble's watchword was—Destroy,
And blazing London seem'd a second Troy;
Liberty blush'd, and hung her drooping head,
Beheld their progress with the deepest dread;
Blush'd that effects like these she should produce,
Worse than the deeds of galley-slaves broke loose.
She loses in such storms her very name,
And fierce licentiousness should bear the blame.
  Incomparable gem! thy worth untold;
Cheap, though blood-bought, and thrown away when sold;
May no foes ravish thee, and no false friend
Betray thee, while professing to defend!
Prize it, ye ministers; ye monarchs, spare;
Ye patriots, guard it with a miser's care.

A. Patriots, alas! the few that have been found,
Where most they flourish, upon English ground,
The country's need have scantily supplied,

And the last left the scene when Chatham died.

B. Not so—the virtue still adorns our age,
Though the chief actor died upon the stage.
In him Demosthenes was heard again;
Liberty taught him her Athenian strain;
She clothed him with authority and awe,
Spoke from his lips, and in his looks gave law.
His speech, his form, his action, full of grace,
And all his country beaming in his face,
He stood, as some inimitable hand
Would strive to make a Paul or Tully stand.
No sycophant or slave, that dared oppose
Her sacred cause, but trembled when he rose;
And every venal stickler for the yoke
Felt himself crushed at the first word he spoke.

   Such men are raised to station and command,
When Providence means mercy to a land.
He speaks, and they appear; to him they owe
Skill to direct, and strength to strike the blow;
To manage with address, to seize with power
The crisis of a dark decisive hour.
So Gideon earned a victory not his own;
Subserviency his praise, and that alone.

   Poor England! thou art a devoted deer,
Beset with every ill but that of fear.
The nations hunt; all mark thee for a prey;
They swarm around thee, and thou stand'st at bay:
Undaunted still, though wearied and perplex'd,
Once Chatham saved thee; but who saves thee next?
Alas! the tide of pleasure sweeps along
All that should be the boast of British song.
'Tis not the wreath that once adorn'd thy brow,
The prize of happier times, will serve thee now.
Our ancestry, a gallant Christian race,
Patterns of every virtue, every grace,
Confess'd a God; they kneel'd before they fought,
And praised him in the victories he wrought.
Now from the dust of ancient days bring forth
Their sober zeal, integrity, and worth;
Courage, ungraced by these, affronts the skies,
Is but the fire without the sacrifice.
The stream that feeds the wellspring of the heart
Not more invigorates life's noblest part,
Than virtue quickens with a warmth divine
The powers that sin has brought to a decline.

A. The inestimable estimate of Brown

Rose like a paper-kite, and charm'd the town;
But measures, plann'd and executed well,
Shifted the wind that raised it, and it fell.
He trod the very selfsame ground you tread,
And victory refuted all he said.

B. And yet his judgment was not framed amiss;
Its error, if it err'd, was merely this—
He thought the dying hour already come,
And a complete recovery struck him dumb.
But that effeminacy, folly, lust,
Enervate and enfeeble, and needs must;
And that a nation shamefully debased
Will be despised and trampled on at last,
Unless sweet penitence her powers renew,
Is truth, if history itself be true.
There is a time, and justice marks the date,
For long forbearing clemency to wait;
That hour elapsed, the incurable revolt
Is punish'd, and down comes the thunderbolt.
If Mercy then put by the threatening blow,
Must she perform the same kind office now?
May she! and, if offended Heaven be still
Accessible, and prayer prevail, she will.
'Tis not, however, insolence and noise,
The tempest of tumultuary joys,
Nor is it yet despondence and dismay
Will win her visits or engage her stay;
Prayer only, and the penitential tear,
Can call her smiling down, and fix her here.
   But when a country (one that I could name)
In prostitution sinks the sense of shame;
When infamous venality, grown bold,
Writes on his bosom, to be let or sold;
When perjury, that Heaven-defying vice,
Sells oaths by tale, and at the lowest price,
Stamps God's own name upon a lie just made,
To turn a penny in the way of trade;
When avarice starves (and never hides his face)
Two or three millions of the human race,
And not a tongue inquires how, where, or when,
Though conscience will have twinges now and then:
When profanation of the sacred cause
In all its parts, times, ministry, and laws,
Bespeaks a land, once Christian, fallen and lost,
In all that wars against that title most;
What follows next let cities of great name,
And regions long since desolate proclaim.

Nineveh, Babylon, and ancient Rome
Speak to the present times and times to come;
They cry aloud in every careless ear,
Stop, while ye may; suspend your mad career;
O learn, from our example and our fate,
Learn wisdom and repentance ere too late!
   Not only Vice disposes and prepares
The mind that slumbers sweetly in her snares,
To stoop to tyranny's usurped command,
And bend her polish'd neck beneath his hand
(A dire effect, by one of Nature's laws
Unchangeably connected with its cause);
But Providence himself will intervene,
To throw his dark displeasure o'er the scene.
All are his instruments; each form of war,
What burns at home, or threatens from afar,
Nature in arms, her elements at strife,
The storms that overset the joys of life,
Are but his rods to scourge a guilty land,
And waste it at the bidding of his hand.
He gives the word, and mutiny soon roars
In all her gates, and shakes her distant shores;
The standards of all nations are unfurl'd;
She has one foe, and that one foe the world.
And if he doom that people with a frown,
And mark them with a seal of wrath press'd down,
Obduracy takes place; callous and tough,
The reprobated race grows judgment-proof:
Earth shakes beneath them, and Heaven roars above;
But nothing scares them from the course they love.
To the lascivious pipe and wanton song,
That charm down fear, they frolic it along,
With mad rapidity and unconcern,
Down to the gulf from which is no return.
They trust in navies, and their navies fail—
God's curse can cast away ten thousand sail!
They trust in armies, and their courage dies;
In wisdom, wealth, in fortune, and in lies;
But all they trust in withers, as it must,
When He commands in whom they place no trust.
Vengeance at last pours down upon their coast
A long despised, but now victorious, host;
Tyranny sends the chain that must abridge
The noble sweep of all their privilege;
Gives liberty the last, the mortal, shock;
Slips the slave's collar on, and snaps the lock.

A. Such lofty strains embellish what you teach,

Mean you to prophesy, or but to preach?

B. I know the mind that feels indeed the fire
The Muse imparts, and can command the lyre,
Acts with a force, and kindles with a zeal,
Whatever the theme, that others never feel.
If human woes her soft attention claim,
A tender sympathy pervades the frame,
She pours a sensibility divine
Along the nerve of every feeling line.
But if a deed not tamely to be borne
Fire indignation and a sense of scorn,
The strings are swept with such a power, so loud,
The storm of music shakes the astonish'd crowd.
So, when remote futurity is brought
Before the keen inquiry of her thought,
A terrible sagacity informs
The poet's heart; he looks to distant storms;
He hears the thunder ere the tempest lowers!
And, arm'd with strength surpassing human powers,
Seizes events as yet unknown to man,
And darts his soul into the dawning plan.
Hence, in a Roman mouth, the graceful name
Of prophet and of poet was the same;
Hence British poets too the priesthood shared,
And every hallowed druid was a bard.
But no prophetic fires to me belong;
I play with syllables, and sport in song.

A. At Westminster, where little poets strive
To set a distich upon six and five,
Where Discipline helps opening buds of sense
And makes his pupils proud with silver pence,
I was a poet too: but modern taste
Is so refined, and delicate, and chaste,
That verse, whatever fire the fancy warms,
Without a creamy smoothness has no charms.
Thus all success depending on an ear,
And thinking I might purchase it too dear,
If sentiment were sacrificed to sound,
And truth cut short to make a period round,
I judged a man of sense could scarce do worse
Than caper in the morris-dance of verse.

B. Thus reputation is a spur to wit,
And some wits flag through fear of losing it,
Give me the line that ploughs its stately course,
Like a proud swan, conquering the stream by force;

That, like some cottage beauty, strikes the heart,
Quite unindebted to the tricks of art.
When labour and when dullness, club in hand,
Like the two figures at St. Dunstan's stand,
Beating alternately, in measured time,
The clockwork tintinnabulum of rhyme,
Exact and regular the sounds will be;
But such mere quarter-strokes are not for me.
   From him who rears a poem lank and long,
To him who strains his all into a song;
Perhaps some bonny Caledonian air,
All birks and braes, though he was never there;
Or, having whelp'd a prologue with great pains,
Feels himself spent, and fumbles for his brains;
A prologue interdash'd with many a stroke—
An art contriv'd to advertise a joke,
So that the jest is clearly to be seen,
Not in the words—but in the gap between;
Manner is all in all, whate'er is writ,
The substitute for genius, sense, and wit.
   To dally much with subjects mean and low
Proves that the mind is weak, or makes it so.
Neglected talents rust into decay,
And every effort ends in pushpin play
The man that means success should soar above
A soldier's feather, or a lady's glove;
Else, summoning the muse to such a theme,
The fruit of all her labour is whipp'd cream.
As if an eagle flew aloft, and then—
Stoop'd from its highest pitch to pounce a wren.
As if the poet, purposing to wed,
Should carve himself a wife in gingerbread.
   Ages elaps'd ere Homer's lamp appear'd,
And ages ere the Mantuan swan was heard;
To carry nature lengths unknown before,
To give a Milton birth, ask'd ages more.
Thus genius rose and set at order'd times,
And shot a day-spring into distant climes,
Ennobling every region that he chose;
He sunk in Greece, in Italy he rose;
And, tedious years of Gothic darkness pass'd,
Emerged all splendour in our isle at last.
Thus lovely halcyons dive into the main,
Then show far off their shining plumes again.

A. Is genius only found in epic lays?
Prove this, and forfeit all pretence to praise.
Make their heroic powers your own at once,

Or candidly confess yourself a dunce.

B. These were the chief; each interval of night
Was graced with many an undulating light.
In less illustrious bards his beauty shone
A meteor, or a star; in these, the sun.
   The nightingale may claim the topmost bough,
While the poor grasshopper must chirp below.
Like him unnoticed, I, and such as I,
Spread little wings, and rather skip than fly;
Perch'd on the meagre produce of the land,
An ell or two of prospect we command;
But never peep beyond the thorny bound,
Or oaken fence, that hems the paddock round.
   In Eden, ere yet innocence of heart
Had faded, poetry was not an art;
Language, above all teaching, or if taught,
Only by gratitude and glowing thought,
Elegant as simplicity, and warm
As ecstacy, unmanacled by form,
Not prompted, as in our degenerate days,
By low ambition and the thirst of praise,
Was natural as is the flowing stream,
And yet magnificent—a God the theme!
That theme on earth exhausted, though above
'Tis found as everlasting as his love,
Man lavish'd all his thoughts on human things—
The feats of heroes and the wrath of kings;
But still, while virtue kindled his delight,
The song was moral, and so far was right.
'Twas thus till luxury seduced the mind
To joys less innocent, as less refined;
Then Genius danced a bacchanal; he crown'd
The brimming goblet, seized the thyrsus, bound
His brows with ivy, rush'd into the field
Of wild imagination, and there reel'd,
The victim of his own lascivious fires,
And, dizzy with delight, profaned the sacred wires:
Anacreon, Horace, play'd in Greece and Rome
This bedlam part; and others nearer home.
When Cromwell fought for power, and while he reign'd
The proud protector of the power he gain'd,
Religion, harsh, intolerant, austere,
Parent of manners like herself severe,
Drew a rough copy of the Christian face,
Without the smile, the sweetness, or the grace;
The dark and sullen humour of the time
Judged every effort of the muse a crime;

Verse, in the finest mould of fancy cast,
Was lumber in an age so void of taste.
But when the second Charles assumed the sway,
And arts revived beneath a softer day,
Then, like a bow long forced into a curve,
The mind, released from too constrain'd a nerve,
Flew to its first position with a spring,
That made the vaulted roofs of pleasure ring.
His court, the dissolute and hateful school
Of wantonness, where vice was taught by rule,
Swarm'd with a scribbling herd, as deep inlaid
With brutal lust as ever Circe made.
From these a long succession, in the rage
Of rank obscenity, debauch'd their age:
Nor ceased till, ever anxious to redress
The abuses of her sacred charge, the press,
The Muse instructed a well nurtured train
Of abler votaries to cleanse the stain,
And claim the palm for purity of song,
That lewdness had usurp'd and worn so long.
Then decent pleasantry and sterling sense,
That neither gave nor would endure offence,
Whipp'd out of sight, with satire just and keen,
The puppy pack that had defiled the scene.
   In front of these came Addison. In him
Humour in holiday and sightly trim,
Sublimity and Attic taste combined,
To polish, furnish, and delight the mind.
Then Pope, as harmony itself exact,
In verse well disciplined, complete, compact,
Gave virtue and morality a grace,
That, quite eclipsing pleasure's painted face,
Levied a tax of wonder and applause,
E'en on the fools that trampled on their laws.
But he (his musical finesse was such,
So nice his ear, so delicate his touch)
Made poetry a mere mechanic art;
And every warbler has his tune by heart.
Nature imparting her satiric gift,
Her serious mirth, to Arbuthnot and Swift,
With droll sobriety they raised a smile
At folly's cost, themselves unmov'd the while
That constellation set, the world in vain
Must hope to look upon their like again.

A. Are we then left?—B. Not wholly in the dark;
Wit now and then, struck smartly, shows a spark,
Sufficient to redeem the modern race

From total night and absolute disgrace.
While servile trick and imitative knack
Confine the million in the beaten track,
Perhaps some courser, who disdains the road,
Snuffs up the wind, and flings himself abroad.
   Contemporaries all surpass'd, see one;
Short his career indeed, but ably run;
Churchill, himself unconscious of his powers,
In penury consumed his idle hours;
And, like a scatter'd seed at random sown,
Was left to spring by vigour of his own.
Lifted at length, by dignity of thought
And dint of genius, to an affluent lot,
He laid his head in luxury's soft lap,
And took, too often, there his easy nap.
If brighter beams than all he threw not forth,
'Twas negligence in him, not want of worth.
Surly and slovenly, and bold and coarse,
Too proud for art, and trusting in mere force,
Spendthrift alike of money and of wit,
Always at speed, and never drawing bit,
He struck the lyre in such a careless mood,
And so disdain'd the rules he understood,
The laurel seem'd to wait on his command;
He snatch'd it rudely from the muses' hand.
Nature, exerting an unwearied power,
Forms, opens, and gives scent to every flower;
Spreads the fresh verdure of the field, and leads
The dancing Naiads through the dewy meads;
She fills profuse ten thousand little throats
With music modulating all their notes;
And charms the woodland scenes and wilds unknown,
With artless airs and concerts of her own:
But seldom (as if fearful of expense)
Vouchsafes to man a poet's just pretence—
Fervency, freedom, fluency of thought,
Harmony, strength, words exquisitely sought;
Fancy, that from the bow that spans the sky
Brings colours, dipp'd in heaven, that never die;
A soul exalted above earth, a mind
Skill'd in the characters that form mankind;
And, as the sun, in rising beauty dress'd,
Looks to the westward from the dappled east,
And marks, whatever clouds may interpose,
Ere yet his race begins, its glorious close;
An eye like his to catch the distant goal;
Or, ere the wheels of verse begin to roll,
Like his to shed illuminating rays

On every scene and subject it surveys:
Thus graced, the man asserts a poet's name,
And the world cheerfully admits the claim.
Pity Religion has so seldom found
A skilful guide into poetic ground!
The flowers would spring where'er she deign'd to stray,
And every muse attend her in her way.
Virtue indeed meets many a rhyming friend,
And many a compliment politely penn'd;
But, unattired in that becoming vest
Religion weaves for her, and half undress'd,
Stands in the desert shivering and forlorn,
A wintry figure, like a wither'd thorn.
The shelves are full, all other themes are sped;
Hackney'd and worn to the last flimsy thread,
Satire has long since done his best; and curst
And loathsome ribaldry has done his worst;
Fancy has sported all her powers away
In tales, in trifles, and in children's play;
And 'tis the sad complaint, and almost true,
Whate'er we write, we bring forth nothing new.
'Twere new indeed to see a bard all fire,
Touch'd with a coal from heaven, assume the lyre,
And tell the world, still kindling as he sung,
With more than mortal music on his tongue,
That He, who died below, and reigns above,
Inspires the song, and that his name is Love.
   For, after all, if merely to beguile,
By flowing numbers and a flowery style,
The tedium that the lazy rich endure,
Which now and then sweet poetry may cure;
Or, if to see the name of idol self,
Stamp'd on the well-bound quarto, grace the shelf,
To float a bubble on the breath of fame,
Prompt his endeavour and engage his aim,
Debased to servile purposes of pride,
How are the powers of genius misapplied!
The gift, whose office is the Giver's praise,
To trace him in his word, his works, his ways!
Then spread the rich discovery, and invite
Mankind to share in the divine delight:
Distorted from its use and just design,
To make the pitiful possessor shine,
To purchase at the fool-frequented fair
Of vanity a wreath for self to wear,
Is profanation of the basest kind—
Proof of a trifling and a worthless mind.

A. Hail, Sternhold, then! and, Hopkins, hail!—B. Amen.
If flattery, folly, lust, employ the pen;
If acrimony, slander, and abuse,
Give it a charge to blacken and traduce;
Though Butler's wit, Pope's numbers, Prior's ease,
With all that fancy can invent to please,
Adorn the polish'd periods as they fall,
One madrigal of theirs is worth them all.

A. 'Twould thin the ranks of the poetic tribe,
To dash the pen through all that you proscribe

B. No matter—we could shift when they were not;
And should, no doubt, if they were all forgot.

THE PROGRESS OF ERROR

Si quid loquar audiendum. Hor. lib. iv. Od. 2.

THE ARGUMENT

Origin of error—Man endowed with freedom of will—Motives for action—Attractions of music—The chase—Those amusements not suited to the Clergy—Case of Occiduus—Force of example—Due observance of the Sabbath—Cards and dancing—The drunkard and the coxcomb—Folly and innocence—Hurtful pleasures—Virtuous pleasures—Effects of the inordinate indulgence of pleasure—Dangerous tendency of many works of imagination—Apostrophe to Lord Chesterfield—Our earliest years the most important—Fashionable education—The grand tour—Accomplishments have taken the place of virtue—Qualities requisite in a critic of the Bible—Power of the press—Solicitude of enthusiasm to make proselytes—Fondness of authors for their literary progeny—The blunderer impatient of contradiction—Moral faults and errors of the understanding reciprocally produce one another—The cup of pleasure to be tasted with caution—Force of habit—The wanderer from the right path directed to the Cross.

Sing, muse (if such a theme, so dark, so long,
May find a muse to grace it with a song),
By what unseen and unsuspected arts
The serpent Error twines round human hearts;
Tell where she lurks, beneath what flowery shades,
That not a glimpse of genuine light pervades,
The poisonous, black, insinuating worm
Successfully conceals her loathsome form.
Take, if ye can, ye careless and supine,
Counsel and caution from a voice like mine!
Truths, that the theorist could never reach,
And observation taught me, I would teach.
   Not all, whose eloquence the fancy fills,
Musical as the chime of tinkling rills,

Weak to perform, though mighty to pretend,
Can trace her mazy windings to their end;
Discern the fraud beneath the specious lure,
Prevent the danger, or prescribe the cure.
The clear harangue, and cold as it is clear,
Falls soporific on the listless ear;
Like quicksilver, the rhetoric they display
Shines as it runs, but, grasp'd at, slips away.

   Placed for his trial on this bustling stage,
From thoughtless youth to ruminating age,
Free in his will to choose or to refuse,
Man may improve the crisis, or abuse;
Else, on the fatalist's unrighteous plan,
Say, to what bar amenable were man?
With nought in charge he could betray no trust:
And, if he fell, would fall because he must;
If love reward him, or if vengeance strike,
His recompence in both unjust alike.
Divine authority within his breast
Brings every thought, word, action, to the test;
Warns him or prompts, approves him or restrains,
As reason, or as passion, takes the reins.
Heaven from above, and conscience from within,
Cries in his startled ear—Abstain from sin!
The world around solicits his desire,
And kindles in his soul a treacherous fire;
While, all his purposes and steps to guard,
Peace follows virtue as its sure reward;
And pleasure brings as surely in her train
Remorse, and sorrow, and vindictive pain.

   Man, thus endued with an elective voice,
Must be supplied with objects of his choice,
Where'er he turns, enjoyment and delight,
Or present or in prospect, meet his sight:
Those open on the spot their honeyed store;
These call him loudly to pursuit of more.
His unexhausted mine the sordid vice
Avarice shows, and virtue is the price.
Here various motives his ambition raise—
Power, pomp, and splendour, and the thirst of praise;
There beauty wooes him with expanded arms;
E'en bacchanalian madness has its charms.

   Nor these alone, whose pleasures less refined
Might well alarm the most unguarded mind,
Seek to supplant his inexperienced youth,
Or lead him devious from the path of truth;
Hourly allurements on his passions press,
Safe in themselves, but dangerous in the excess.

Hark! how it floats upon the dewy air!
O what a dying, dying close was there!
'Tis harmony, from yon sequester'd bower.
Sweet harmony, that soothes the midnight hour!
Long ere the charioteer of day had run
His morning course the enchantment was begun;
And he shall gild yon mountain's height again,
Ere yet the pleasing toil becomes a pain.
    Is this the rugged path, the steep ascent,
That virtue points to? Can a life thus spent
Lead to the bliss she promises the wise,
Detach the soul from earth, and speed her to the skies?
Ye devotees to your adored employ,
Enthusiasts, drunk with an unreal joy,
Love makes the music of the blest above,
Heaven's harmony is universal love;
And earthly sounds, though sweet and well combined,
And lenient as soft opiates to the mind,
Leave vice and folly unsubdued behind.
Grey dawn appears; the sportsman and his train
Speckle the bosom of the distant plain;
'Tis he, the Nimrod of the neighbouring lairs;
Save that his scent is less acute than theirs,
For persevering chase, and headlong leaps,
True beagle as the stanchest hound he keeps.
Charged with the folly of his life's mad scene,
He takes offence, and wonders what you mean;
The joy the danger and the toil o'erpays—
'Tis exercise, and health, and length of days.
Again impetuous to the field he flies;
Leaps every fence but one, there falls and dies;
Like a slain deer, the tumbrel brings him home,
Unmiss'd but by his dogs and by his groom.
    Ye clergy, while your orbit is your place,
Lights of the world and stars of human race;
But, if eccentric ye forsake your sphere,
Prodigies ominous and view'd with fear:
The comet's baneful influence is a dream;
Yours real, and pernicious in the extreme.
What then! are appetites and lusts laid down
With the same ease that man puts on his gown?
Will avarice and concupiscence give place,
Charm'd by the sounds—Your Reverence, or your Grace?
No. But his own engagement binds him fast;
Or, if it does not, brands him to the last
What atheists call him—a designing knave,
A mere church juggler, hypocrite and slave.
Oh, laugh or mourn with me the rueful jest,

A cassock'd huntsman and a fiddling priest!
He from Italian songsters takes his cue:
Set Paul to music, he shall quote him too.
He takes the field. The master of the pack
Cries—Well done, saint! and claps him on the back.
Is this the path of sanctity? Is this
To stand a waymark on the road to bliss?
Himself a wanderer from the narrow way,
His silly sheep, what wonder if they stray?
Go, cast your orders at your bishop's feet,
Send your dishonour'd gown to Monmouth-street!
The sacred function in your hands is made—
Sad sacrilege—no function, but a trade!
   Occiduus is a pastor of renown,
When he has pray'd and preach'd the sabbath down,
With wire and catgut he concludes the day,
Quavering and semiquavering care away.
The full concerto swells upon your ear;
All elbows shake. Look in, and you would swear
The Babylonian tyrant with a nod
Had summon'd them to serve his golden god.
So well that thought the employment seems to suit,
Psaltery and sackbut, dulcimer and flute.
O fie! 'tis evangelical and pure:
Observe each face, how sober and demure!
Ecstacy sets her stamp on every mien;
Chins fallen, and not an eyeball to be seen.
Still I insist, though music heretofore
Has charm'd me much (not e'en Occiduus more),
Love, joy, and peace make harmony more meet
For sabbath evenings, and perhaps as sweet.
   Will not the sickliest sheep of every flock
Resort to this example as a rock;
There stand, and justify the foul abuse
Of sabbath hours with plausible excuse;
If apostolic gravity be free
To play the fool on Sundays, why not we?
If he the tinkling harpsichord regards
As inoffensive, what offence in cards?
Strike up the fiddles, let us all be gay!
Laymen have leave to dance, if parsons play.
   O Italy!—Thy sabbaths will be soon
Our sabbaths, closed with mummery and buffoon.
Preaching and pranks will share the motley scene,
Ours parcelled out, as thine have ever been,
God's worship and the mountebank between.
What says the prophet? Let that day be blest
With holiness and consecrated rest.

Pastime and business, both it should exclude,
And bar the door the moment they intrude;
Nobly distinguished above all the six
By deeds in which the world must never mix.
Hear him again. He calls it a delight,
A day of luxury observed aright,
When the glad soul is made Heaven's welcome guest,
Sits banqueting, and God provides the feast.
But triflers are engaged and cannot come;
Their answer to the call is—Not at home.
   O the dear pleasures of the velvet plain,
The painted tablets, dealt and dealt again!
Cards, with what rapture, and the polish'd die,
The yawning chasm of indolence supply!
Then to the dance, and make the sober moon
Witness of joys that shun the sight of noon.
Blame, cynic, if you can, quadrille or ball,
The snug close party, or the splendid hall,
Where Night, down stooping from her ebon throne,
Views constellations brighter than her own.
'Tis innocent, and harmless, and refined,
The balm of care, Elysium of the mind.
Innocent! Oh, if venerable Time
Slain at the foot of Pleasure be no crime,
Then, with his silver beard and magic wand,
Let Comus rise archbishop of the land;
Let him your rubric and your feasts prescribe,
Grand metropolitan of all the tribe.
   Of manners rough, and coarse athletic cast,
The rank debauch suits Clodio's filthy taste.
Rufillus, exquisitely form'd by rule,
Not of the moral but the dancing school,
Wonders at Clodio's follies, in a tone
As tragical as others at his own.
He cannot drink five bottles, bilk the score,
Then kill a constable, and drink five more;
But he can draw a pattern, make a tart,
And has the ladies' etiquette by heart.
Go, fool; and, arm in arm with Clodio, plead
Your cause before a bar you little dread;
But know, the law that bids the drunkard die
Is far too just to pass the trifler by.
Both baby-featured, and of infant size,
View'd from a distance, and with heedless eyes,
Folly and innocence are so alike,
The difference, though essential, fails to strike.
Yet Folly ever has a vacant stare,
A simpering countenance, and a trifling air;

But Innocence, sedate, serene, erect,
Delights us, by engaging our respect.
Man, Nature's guest by invitation sweet,
Receives from her both appetite and treat;
But, if he play the glutton and exceed,
His benefactress blushes at the deed.
For Nature, nice, as liberal to dispense,
Made nothing but a brute the slave of sense.
Daniel ate pulse by choice—example rare!
Heaven bless'd the youth, and made him fresh and fair.
Gorgonius sits, abdominous and wan,
Like a fat squab upon a Chinese fan:
He snuffs far off the anticipated joy;
Turtle and venison all his thoughts employ;
Prepares for meals as jockeys take a sweat,
Oh, nauseous!—an emetic for a whet!
Will Providence o'erlook the wasted good?
Temperance were no virtue if he could.
That pleasures, therefore, or what such we call,
Are hurtful, is a truth confess'd by all.
And some, that seem to threaten virtue less
Still hurtful in the abuse, or by the excess.
  Is man then only for his torment placed
The centre of delights he may not taste?
Like fabled Tantalus, condemn'd to hear
The precious stream still purling in his ear,
Lip-deep in what he longs for, and yet curst
With prohibition and perpetual thirst?
No, wrangler—destitute of shame and sense,
The precept, that enjoins him abstinence,
Forbids him none but the licentious joy,
Whose fruit, though fair, tempts only to destroy.
Remorse, the fatal egg by Pleasure laid
In every bosom where her nest is made,
Hatch'd by the beams of truth, denies him rest,
And proves a raging scorpion in his breast.
No pleasure? Are domestic comforts dead?
Are all the nameless sweets of friendship fled?
Has time worn out, or fashion put to shame,
Good sense, good health, good conscience, and good fame?
All these belong to virtue, and all prove
That virtue has a title to your love.
Have you no touch of pity, that the poor
Stand starved at your inhospitable door?
Or if yourself, too scantily supplied,
Need help, let honest industry provide.
Earn, if you want; if you abound, impart:
These both are pleasures to the feeling heart.

No pleasure? Has some sickly eastern waste
Sent us a wind to parch us at a blast?
Can British Paradise no scenes afford
To please her sated and indifferent lord?
Are sweet philosophy's enjoyments run
Quite to the lees? And has religion none?
Brutes capable would tell you 'tis a lie,
And judge you from the kennel and the stye.
Delights like these, ye sensual and profane,
Ye are bid, begg'd, besought, to entertain;
Call'd to these crystal streams, do ye turn off
Obscene to swill and swallow at a trough?
Envy the beast, then, on whom Heaven bestows
Your pleasures, with no curses at the close.
   Pleasure admitted in undue degree
Enslaves the will, nor leaves the judgment free.
'Tis not alone the grape's enticing juice
Unnerves the moral powers, and mars their use;
Ambition, avarice, and the lust of fame,
And woman, lovely woman, does the same.
The heart, surrender'd to the ruling power
Of some ungovern'd passion every hour,
Finds by degrees the truths that once bore sway,
And all their deep impressions, wear away;
So coin grows smooth, in traffic current pass'd,
Till Cæsar's image is effaced at last.
   The breach, though small at first, soon opening wide,
In rushes folly with a full-moon tide,
Then welcome errors, of whatever size,
To justify it by a thousand lies.
As creeping ivy clings to wood or stone,
And hides the ruin that it feeds upon;
So sophistry cleaves close to and protects
Sin's rotten trunk, concealing its defects.
Mortals, whose pleasures are their only care,
First wish to be imposed on, and then are.
And lest the fulsome artifice should fail,
Themselves will hide its coarseness with a veil.
Not more industrious are the just and true
To give to Virtue what is Virtue's due—
The praise of wisdom, comeliness, and worth,
And call her charms to public notice forth—
Than Vice's mean and disingenuous race
To hide the shocking features of her face.
Her form with dress and lotion they repair;
Then kiss their idol, and pronounce her fair.
   The sacred implement I now employ
Might prove a mischief, or at best a toy;

A trifle, if it move but to amuse;
But, if to wrong the judgment and abuse,
Worse than a poniard in the basest hand,
It stabs at once the morals of a land.

   Ye writers of what none with safety reads,
Footing it in the dance that Fancy leads;
Ye novelists, who mar what ye would mend,
Snivelling and drivelling folly without end;
Whose corresponding misses fill the ream
With sentimental frippery and dream,
Caught in a delicate soft silken net
By some lewd earl, or rake-hell baronet:
Ye pimps, who, under virtue's fair pretence,
Steal to the closet of young innocence,
And teach her, inexperienced yet and green,
To scribble as you scribbled at fifteen;
Who, kindling a combustion of desire,
With some cold moral think to quench the fire;
Though all your engineering proves in vain
The dribbling stream ne'er puts it out again:
Oh that a verse had power, and could command
Far, far away, these flesh-flies of the land,
Who fasten without mercy on the fair,
And suck, and leave a craving maggot there!
Howe'er disguised the inflammatory tale,
And cover'd with a fine-spun specious veil;
Such writers, and such readers, owe the gust
And relish of their pleasure all to lust.

   But the muse, eagle-pinion'd, has in view
A quarry more important still than you;
Down, down the wind she swims, and sails away,
Now stoops upon it, and now grasps the prey.

   Petronius! all the muses weep for thee;
But every tear shall scald thy memory:
The graces too, while Virtue at their shrine
Lay bleeding under that soft hand of thine,
Felt each a mortal stab in her own breast,
Abhorr'd the sacrifice, and cursed the priest.
Thou polish'd and high-finish'd foe to truth,
Graybeard corrupter of our listening youth,
To purge and skim away the filth of vice,
That so refined it might the more entice,
Then pour it on the morals of thy son,
To taint his heart, was worthy of thine own!
Now, while the poison all high life pervades,
Write, if thou canst, one letter from the shades,
One, and one only, charged with deep regret,
That thy worst part, thy principles, live yet;

One sad epistle thence may cure mankind
Of the plague spread by bundles left behind.
   'Tis granted, and no plainer truth appears,
Our most important are our earliest years;
The mind, impressible and soft, with ease
Imbibes and copies what she hears and sees,
And through life's labyrinth holds fast the clue
That Education gives her, false or true.
Plants raised with tenderness are seldom strong;
Man's coltish disposition asks the thong;
And without discipline the favourite child,
Like a neglected forester, runs wild.
But we, as if good qualities would grow
Spontaneous, take but little pains to sow:
We give some Latin and a smatch of Greek;
Teach him to fence and figure twice a week;
And having done, we think, the best we can,
Praise his proficiency, and dub him man.
   From school to Cam or Isis, and thence home;
And thence with all convenient speed to Rome,
With reverend tutor, clad in habit lay,
To tease for cash, and quarrel with all day;
With memorandum book for every town,
And every post, and where the chaise broke down;
His stock, a few French phrases got by heart,
With much to learn, but nothing to impart;
The youth, obedient to his sire's commands,
Sets off a wanderer into foreign lands.
Surprised at all they meet, the gosling pair,
With awkward gait, stretch'd neck, and silly stare,
Discover huge cathedrals built with stone,
And steeples towering high, much like our own;
But show peculiar light by many a grin
At popish practices observed within.
   Ere long some bowing, smirking, smart abbé
Remarks two loiterers that have lost their way;
And, being always primed with politesse
For men of their appearance and address,
With much compassion undertakes the task
To tell them more than they have wit to ask;
Points to inscriptions wheresoe'er they tread,
Such as, when legible, were never read,
But being canker'd now and half worn out,
Craze antiquarian brains with endless doubt;
Some headless hero, or some Cæsar shows—
Defective only in his Roman nose;
Exhibits elevations, drawings, plans,
Models of Herculanum pots and pans;

And sells them medals, which, if neither rare
Nor ancient, will be so, preserved with care.
  Strange the recital! from whatever cause
His great improvement and new lights he draws,
The squire, once bashful, is shamefaced no more,
But teems with powers he never felt before;
Whether increased momentum, and the force
With which from clime to clime he sped his course,
(As axles sometimes kindle as they go,)
Chafed him, and brought dull nature to a glow;
Or whether clearer skies and softer air,
That make Italian flowers so sweet and fair,
Freshening his lazy spirits as he ran,
Unfolded genially, and spread the man;
Returning, he proclaims, by many a grace,
By shrugs and strange contortions of his face,
How much a dunce, that has been sent to roam,
Excels a dunce that has been kept at home.
  Accomplishments have taken virtue's place,
And wisdom falls before exterior grace:
We slight the precious kernel of the stone,
And toil to polish its rough coat alone.
A just deportment, manners graced with ease,
Elegant phrase, and figure form'd to please,
Are qualities that seem to comprehend
Whatever parents, guardians, schools, intend;
Hence an unfurnish'd and a listless mind,
Though busy, trifling; empty, though refined;
Hence all that interferes, and dares to clash
With indolence and luxury, is trash;
While learning, once the man's exclusive pride,
Seems verging fast towards the female side.
Learning itself, received into a mind
By nature weak, or viciously inclined,
Serves but to lead philosophers astray,
Where children would with ease discern the way.
And of all arts sagacious dupes invent,
To cheat themselves and gain the world's assent,
The worst is—Scripture warp'd from its intent.
  The carriage bowls along, and all are pleased
If Tom be sober, and the wheels well greased;
But if the rogue be gone a cup too far,
Left out his linchpin, or forgot his tar,
It suffers interruption and delay,
And meets with hindrance in the smoothest way.
When some hypothesis absurd and vain
Has fill'd with all its fumes a critic's brain,
The text that sorts not with his darling whim,

Though plain to others, is obscure to him.
The will made subject to a lawless force,
All is irregular, and out of course;
And Judgment drunk, and bribed to lose his way,
Winks hard, and talks of darkness at noonday.
    A critic on the sacred book should be
Candid and learn'd, dispassionate and free;
Free from the wayward bias bigots feel,
From fancy's influence, and intemperate zeal;
But above all, (or let the wretch refrain,
Nor touch the page he cannot but profane,)
Free from the domineering power of lust;
A lewd interpreter is never just.
    How shall I speak thee, or thy power address,
Thou god of our idolatry, the Press?
By thee religion, liberty, and laws,
Exert their influence and advance their cause:
By thee worse plagues than Pharaoh's land befell,
Diffused, make Earth the vestibule of Hell;
Thou fountain, at which drink the good and wise,
Thou ever-bubbling spring of endless lies;
Like Eden's dread probationary tree,
Knowledge of good and evil is from thee!
    No wild enthusiast ever yet could rest
Till half mankind were like himself possess'd.
Philosophers, who darken and put out
Eternal truth by everlasting doubt;
Church quacks, with passions under no command,
Who fill the world with doctrines contraband,
Discoverers of they know not what, confined
Within no bounds—the blind that lead the blind;
To streams of popular opinion drawn,
Deposit in those shallows all their spawn.
The wriggling fry soon fill the creeks around,
Poisoning the waters where their swarms abound.
Scorn'd by the nobler tenants of the flood,
Minnows and gudgeons gorge the unwholesome food.
The propagated myriads spread so fast,
E'en Leuwenhoeck himself would stand aghast,
Employ'd to calculate the enormous sum,
And own his crab-computing powers o'ercome.
Is this hyperbole? The world well known,
Your sober thoughts will hardly find it one.
    Fresh confidence the speculatist takes
From every hair-brain'd proselyte he makes;
And therefore prints: himself but half deceived,
Till others have the soothing tale believed.
Hence comment after comment, spun as fine

As bloated spiders draw the flimsy line.
Hence the same word that bids our lusts obey
Is misapplied to sanctify their sway.
If stubborn Greek refuse to be his friend,
Hebrew or Syriac shall be forced to bend;
If languages and copies all cry, No—
Somebody proved it centuries ago.
Like trout pursued, the critic in despair
Darts to the mud, and finds his safety there:
Women, whom custom has forbid to fly
The scholar's pitch, (the scholar best knows why,)
With all the simple and unletter'd poor,
Admire his learning, and almost adore.
Whoever errs, the priest can ne'er be wrong,
With such fine words familiar to his tongue.

   Ye ladies! (for, indifferent in your cause,
I should deserve to forfeit all applause)
Whatever shocks or gives the least offence
To virtue, delicacy, truth, or sense,
(Try the criterion, 'tis a faithful guide,)
Nor has, nor can have, Scripture on its side.

   None but an author knows an author's cares,
Or Fancy's fondness for the child she bears.
Committed once into the public arms,
The baby seems to smile with added charms.
Like something precious ventured far from shore,
'Tis valued for the danger's sake the more.
He views it with complacency supreme,
Solicits kind attention to his dream;
And daily, more enamour'd of the cheat,
Kneels, and asks Heaven to bless the dear deceit.
So one, whose story serves at least to show
Men loved their own productions long ago,
Wooed an unfeeling statue for his wife,
Nor rested till the gods had given it life.
If some mere driveller suck the sugar'd fib,
One that still needs his leading string and bib,
And praise his genius, he is soon repaid
In praise applied to the same part—his head;
For 'tis a rule that holds for ever true,
Grant me discernment, and I grant it you.

   Patient of contradiction as a child,
Affable, humble, diffident, and mild;
Such was Sir Isaac, and such Boyle and Locke;
Your blunderer is as sturdy as a rock.
The creature is so sure to kick and bite,
A muleteer's the man to set him right.
First Appetite enlists him Truth's sworn foe,

Then obstinate Self-will confirms him so.
Tell him he wanders; that his error leads
To fatal ills; that, though the path he treads
Be flowery, and he see no cause of fear,
Death and the pains of hell attend him there:
In vain; the slave of arrogance and pride,
He has no hearing on the prudent side.
His still refuted quirks he still repeats;
New raised objections with new quibbles meets;
Till, sinking in the quicksand he defends,
He dies disputing, and the contest ends—
But not the mischiefs; they, still left behind,
Like thistle-seeds, are sown by every wind.

   Thus men go wrong with an ingenious skill;
Bend the straight rule to their own crooked will;
And, with a clear and shining lamp supplied,
First put it out, then take it for a guide.
Halting on crutches of unequal size,
One leg by truth supported, one by lies,
They sidle to the goal with awkward pace,
Secure of nothing—but to lose the race.

   Faults in the life breed errors in the brain,
And these reciprocally those again.
The mind and conduct mutually imprint
And stamp their image in each other's mint;
Each, sire and dam of an infernal race,
Begetting and conceiving all that's base.

   None sends his arrow to the mark in view,
Whose hand is feeble, or his aim untrue.
For though, ere yet the shaft is on the wing,
Or when it first forsakes the elastic string,
It err but little from the intended line,
It falls at last far wide of his design;
So he who seeks a mansion in the sky,
Must watch his purpose with a stedfast eye;
That prize belongs to none but the sincere,
The least obliquity is fatal here.

   With caution taste the sweet Circean cup;
He that sips often, at last drinks it up.
Habits are soon assumed; but when we strive
To strip them off, 'tis being flay'd alive.
Call'd to the temple of impure delight,
He that abstains, and he alone, does right.
If a wish wander that way, call it home;
He cannot long be safe whose wishes roam.
But if you pass the threshold, you are caught;
Die then, if power Almighty save you not.
There hardening by degrees, till double steel'd,

Take leave of nature's God, and God reveal'd;
Then laugh at all you trembled at before;
And, joining the freethinkers' brutal roar,
Swallow the two grand nostrums they dispense—
That Scripture lies, and blasphemy is sense.
If clemency revolted by abuse
Be damnable, then damn'd without excuse.
    Some dream that they can silence, when they will,
The storm of passion, and say, Peace, be still:
But "Thus far and no farther," when address'd
To the wild wave, or wilder human breast,
Implies authority that never can,
That never ought to be the lot of man.
    But, muse, forbear; long flights forebode a fall;
Strike on the deep-toned chord the sum of all.
    Hear the just law—the judgment of the skies!
He that hates truth shall be the dupe of lies;
And he that will be cheated to the last,
Delusions strong as hell shall bind him fast.
But if the wanderer his mistake discern,
Judge his own ways, and sigh for a return,
Bewilder'd once, must he bewail his loss
For ever and for ever? No—the cross!
There and there only (though the deist rave,
And atheist, if Earth bear so base a slave);
There and there only is the power to save.
There no delusive hope invites despair;
No mockery meets you, no deception there.
The spells and charms, that blinded you before,
All vanish there, and fascinate no more.
    I am no preacher, let this hint suffice—
The cross once seen is death to every vice;
Else He that hung there suffer'd all his pain,
Bled, groan'd, and agonized, and died, in vain.

TRUTH

Pensantur trutinâ. Hor. lib. ii. Ep. 1.

THE ARGUMENT

The pursuit of error leads to destruction—Grace leads the right way—Its direction despised—The self-sufficient Pharisee compared with the peacock—The pheasant compared with the Christian—Heaven abhors affected sanctity—The hermit and his penances—The self-torturing Bramin—Pride the ruling principle of both—Picture of a sanctimonious prude—Picture of a saint—Freedom of a Christian—Importance of motives, illustrated by the conduct of two servants—The traveller overtaken by a storm

Man, on the dubious waves of error toss'd,
His ship half founder'd, and his compass lost,
Sees, far as human optics may command,
A sleeping fog, and fancies it dry land;
Spreads all his canvas, every sinew plies;
Pants for it, aims at it, enters it, and dies!
Then farewell all self-satisfying schemes,
His well-built systems, philosophic dreams;
Deceitful views of future bliss, farewell!
He reads his sentence at the flames of hell.
   Hard lot of man—to toil for the reward
Of virtue, and yet lose it! Wherefore hard?—
He that would win the race must guide his horse
Obedient to the customs of the course;
Else, though unequall'd to the goal he flies,
A meaner than himself shall gain the prize.
Grace leads the right way: if you choose the wrong,
Take it and perish; but restrain your tongue;
Charge not, with light sufficient and left free,
Your wilful suicide on God's decree.
   Oh how unlike the complex works of man,
Heav'n's easy, artless, unencumber'd plan!
No meretricious graces to beguile,
No clustering ornaments to clog the pile;
From ostentation, as from weakness, free,
It stands like the cerulian arch we see,
Majestic in its own simplicity.
Inscribed above the portal, from afar
Conspicuous as the brightness of a star,
Legible only by the light they give,
Stand the soul-quickening words—BELIEVE, AND LIVE.
Too many, shock'd at what should charm them most,
Despise the plain direction, and are lost.
Heaven on such terms! (they cry with proud disdain)
Incredible, impossible, and vain!—
Rebel, because 'tis easy to obey;
And scorn, for its own sake, the gracious way.
These are the sober, in whose cooler brains
Some thought of immortality remains;
The rest too busy or too gay to wait

On the sad theme, their everlasting state,
Sport for a day, and perish in a night;
The foam upon the waters not so light.
   Who judged the Pharisee! What odious cause
Exposed him to the vengeance of the laws?
Had he seduced a virgin, wrong'd a friend,
Or stabb'd a man to serve some private end?
Was blasphemy his sin? Or did he stray
From the strict duties of the sacred day?
Sit long and late at the carousing board?
(Such were the sins with which he charged his Lord.)
No—the man's morals were exact. What then?
'Twas his ambition to be seen of men;
His virtues were his pride; and that one vice
Made all his virtues gewgaws of no price;
He wore them as fine trappings for a show,
A praying, synagogue-frequenting beau.
   The self-applauding bird, the peacock, see—
Mark what a sumptuous pharisee is he!
Meridian sunbeams tempt him to unfold
His radiant glories, azure, green, and gold:
He treads as if, some solemn music near,
His measured step were govern'd by his ear;
And seems to say—Ye meaner fowl give place;
I am all splendour, dignity, and grace!
   Not so the pheasant on his charms presumes,
Though he, too, has a glory in his plumes.
He, Christian-like, retreats with modest mien
To the close copse or far sequester'd green,
And shines without desiring to be seen.
The plea of works, as arrogant and vain,
Heaven turns from with abhorrence and disdain;
Not more affronted by avow'd neglect,
Than by the mere dissembler's feign'd respect.
What is all righteousness that men devise?
What—but a sordid bargain for the skies?
But Christ as soon would abdicate his own,
As stoop from heaven to sell the proud a throne.
   His dwelling a recess in some rude rock;
Book, beads, and maple dish, his meagre stock;
In shirt of hair and weeds of canvas dress'd,
Girt with a bell-rope that the pope has bless'd;
Adust with stripes told out for every crime,
And sore tormented, long before his time;
His prayer preferr'd to saints that cannot aid,
His praise postponed, and never to be paid;
See the sage hermit, by mankind admired,
With all that bigotry adopts inspired,

Wearing out life in his religious whim,
Till his religious whimsy wears out him.
His works, his abstinence, his zeal allow'd,
You think him humble—God accounts him proud.
High in demand, though lowly in pretence,
Of all his conduct this the genuine sense—
My penitential stripes, my streaming blood,
Have purchased heaven, and proved my title good.
   Turn eastward now, and fancy shall apply
To your weak sight her telescopic eye.
The bramin kindles on his own bare head
The sacred fire, self-torturing his trade!
His voluntary pains, severe and long,
Would give a barbarous air to British song;
No grand inquisitor could worse invent,
Than he contrives to suffer well content.
   Which is the saintlier worthy of the two?
Past all dispute, yon anchorite, say you.
Your sentence and mine differ. What's a name?
I say the bramin has the fairer claim.
If sufferings scripture nowhere recommends,
Devised by self, to answer selfish ends,
Give saintship, then all Europe must agree
Ten starveling hermits suffer less than he.
The truth is (if the truth may suit your ear,
And prejudice have left a passage clear)
Pride has attained a most luxuriant growth,
And poison'd every virtue in them both.
Pride may be pamper'd while the flesh grows lean;
Humility may clothe an English dean;
That grace was Cowper's—his, confess'd by all—
Though placed in golden Durham's second stall.
Not all the plenty of a bishop's board,
His palace, and his lacqueys, and "My Lord,"
More nourish pride, that condescending vice,
Than abstinence, and beggary, and lice;
It thrives in misery, and abundant grows:
In misery fools upon themselves impose.
   But why before us protestants produce
An Indian mystic or a French recluse?
Their sin is plain; but what have we to fear,
Reform'd and well-instructed? You shall hear.
   Yon ancient prude, whose wither'd features show
She might be young some forty years ago,
Her elbows pinioned close upon her hips,
Her head erect, her fan upon her lips,
Her eyebrows arched, her eyes both gone astray
To watch yon amorous couple in their play,

With bony and unkerchief'd neck defies
The rude inclemency of wintry skies,
And sails with lappet head and mincing airs
Duly at clink of bell to morning prayers.
To thrift and parsimony much inclined,
She yet allows herself that boy behind;
The shivering urchin, bending as he goes,
With slipshod heels and dewdrop at his nose,
His predecessor's coat advanced to wear,
Which future pages yet are doom'd to share,
Carries her Bible tuck'd beneath his arm,
And hides his hands to keep his fingers warm.

   She, half an angel in her own account,
Doubts not hereafter with the saints to mount,
Though not a grace appears on strictest search,
But that she fasts, and item, goes to church.
Conscious of age, she recollects her youth,
And tells, not always with an eye to truth,
Who spann'd her waist, and who, where'er he came,
Scrawl'd upon glass Miss Bridget's lovely name;
Who stole her slipper, fill'd it with tokay,
And drank the little bumper every day.
Of temper as envenom'd as an asp,
Censorious, and her every word a wasp;
In faithful memory she records the crimes
Or real, or fictitious, of the times;
Laughs at the reputations she has torn,
And holds them dangling at arm's length in scorn.

   Such are the fruits of sanctimonious pride,
Of malice fed while flesh is mortified:
Take, madam, the reward of all your prayers,
Where hermits and where bramins meet with theirs;
Your portion is with them.—Nay, never frown,
But, if you please, some fathoms lower down.

   Artist, attend—your brushes and your paint—
Produce them—take a chair—now draw a saint.
Oh sorrowful and sad! the streaming tears
Channel her cheeks—a Niobe appears!
Is this a saint? Throw tints and all away—
True piety is cheerful as the day,
Will weep indeed and heave a pitying groan
For others' woes, but smiles upon her own.

   What purpose has the King of saints in view?
Why falls the gospel like a gracious dew?
To call up plenty from the teeming earth,
Or curse the desert with a tenfold dearth?
Is it that Adam's offspring may be saved
From servile fear, or be the more enslaved?

To loose the links that gall'd mankind before,
Or bind them faster on, and add still more?
The freeborn Christian has no chains to prove,
Or, if a chain, the golden one of love:
No fear attends to quench his glowing fires,
What fear he feels his gratitude inspires.
Shall he, for such deliverance freely wrought,
Recompense ill? He trembles at the thought.
His Master's interest and his own combined
Prompt every movement of his heart and mind:
Thought, word, and deed, his liberty evince,
His freedom is the freedom of a prince.

   Man's obligations infinite, of course
His life should prove that he perceives their force;
His utmost he can render is but small—
The principle and motive all in all.
You have two servants—Tom, an arch, sly rogue,
From top to toe the Geta now in vogue,
Genteel in figure, easy in address,
Moves without noise, and swift as an express,
Reports a message with a pleasing grace,
Expert in all the duties of his place;
Say, on what hinge does his obedience move?
Has he a world of gratitude and love?
No, not a spark—'tis all mere sharper's play;
He likes your house, your housemaid, and your pay;
Reduce his wages, or get rid of her,
Tom quits you, with—Your most obedient, sir.

   The dinner served, Charles takes his usual stand,
Watches your eye, anticipates command;
Sighs, if perhaps your appetite should fail;
And, if he but suspects a frown, turns pale;
Consults all day your interest and your ease,
Richly rewarded if he can but please;
And, proud to make his firm attachment known,
To save your life would nobly risk his own.

   Now which stands highest in your serious thought?
Charles, without doubt, say you—and so he ought;
One act, that from a thankful heart proceeds,
Excels ten thousand mercenary deeds.

   Thus Heaven approves as honest and sincere
The work of generous love and filial fear;
But with averted eyes the omniscient Judge
Scorns the base hireling and the slavish drudge.

   Where dwell these matchless saints? old Curio cries.
E'en at your side, sir, and before your eyes,
The favour'd few—the enthusiasts you despise.
And, pleased at heart because on holy ground,

Sometimes a canting hypocrite is found,
Reproach a people with his single fall,
And cast his filthy raiment at them all.
Attend! an apt similitude shall show
Whence springs the conduct that offends you so.
  See where it smokes along the sounding plain,
Blown all aslant, a driving, dashing rain,
Peal upon peal redoubling all around,
Shakes it again and faster to the ground;
Now flashing wide, now glancing as in play,
Swift beyond thought the lightnings dart away.
Ere yet it came the traveller urged his steed,
And hurried, but with unsuccessful speed;
Now drench'd throughout, and hopeless of his case,
He drops the rein, and leaves him to his pace.
Suppose, unlook'd for in a scene so rude,
Long hid by interposing hill or wood,
Some mansion, neat and elegantly dress'd,
By some kind hospitable heart possess'd,
Offer him warmth, security, and rest;
Think with what pleasure, safe, and at his ease,
He hears the tempest howling in the trees;
What glowing thanks his lips and heart employ,
While danger past is turn'd to present joy.
So fares it with the sinner, when he feels
A growing dread of vengeance at his heels:
His conscience like a glassy lake before,
Lash'd into foaming waves, begins to roar;
The law, grown clamorous, though silent long,
Arraigns him, charges him with every wrong—
Asserts the right of his offended Lord,
And death, or restitution, is the word:
The last impossible, he fears the first,
And, having well deserved, expects the worst.
Then welcome refuge and a peaceful home;
Oh for a shelter from the wrath to come!
Crush me, ye rocks; ye falling mountains, hide,
Or bury me in ocean's angry tide!—
The scrutiny of those all-seeing eyes
I dare not—And you need not, God replies;
The remedy you want I freely give;
The book shall teach you—read, believe, and live!
'Tis done—the raging storm is heard no more,
Mercy receives him on her peaceful shore:
And Justice, guardian of the dread command,
Drops the red vengeance from his willing hand.
A soul redeem'd demands a life of praise;
Hence the complexion of his future days,

Hence a demeanour holy and unspeck'd,
And the world's hatred, as its sure effect.
　　Some lead a life unblameable and just,
Their own dear virtue their unshaken trust:
They never sin—or if (as all offend)
Some trivial slips their daily walk attend,
The poor are near at hand, the charge is small,
A slight gratuity atones for all.
For though the pope has lost his interest here,
And pardons are not sold as once they were,
No papist more desirous to compound,
Than some grave sinners upon English ground.
That plea refuted, other quirks they seek—
Mercy is infinite, and man is weak;
The future shall obliterate the past,
And heaven, no doubt, shall be their home at last.
　　Come, then—a still, small whisper in your ear—
He has no hope who never had a fear;
And he that never doubted of his state,
He may perhaps—perhaps he may—too late.
　　The path to bliss abounds with many a snare;
Learning is one, and wit, however rare.
The Frenchman, first in literary fame,
(Mention him, if you please. Voltaire?—The same)
With spirit, genius, eloquence, supplied,
Lived long, wrote much, laugh'd heartily, and died;
The Scripture was his jest book, whence he drew
Bon-mots to gall the Christian and the Jew;
An infidel in health, but what when sick?
Oh—then a text would touch him at the quick;
View him at Paris in his last career,
Surrounding throngs the demi-god revere;
Exalted on his pedestal of pride,
And fumed with frankincense on every side,
He begs their flattery with his latest breath,
And, smother'd in't at last, is praised to death!
　　Yon cottager, who weaves at her own door,
Pillow and bobbins all her little store;
Content though mean, and cheerful if not gay,
Shuffling her threads about the live-long day,
Just earns a scanty pittance, and at night
Lies down secure, her heart and pocket light;
She, for her humble sphere by nature fit,
Has little understanding, and no wit,
Receives no praise; but though her lot be such,
(Toilsome and indigent,) she renders much;
Just knows, and knows no more, her Bible true—
A truth the brilliant Frenchman never knew;

And in that charter reads with sparkling eyes,
Her title to a treasure in the skies.
Oh, happy peasant! Oh, unhappy bard!
His the mere tinsel, hers the rich reward;
He praised perhaps for ages yet to come,
She never heard of half a mile from home:
He, lost in errors, his vain heart prefers,
She, safe in the simplicity of hers.
   Not many wise, rich, noble, or profound
In science win one inch of heavenly ground.
And is it not a mortifying thought
The poor should gain it, and the rich should not?
No—the voluptuaries, who ne'er forget
One pleasure lost, lose heaven without regret;
Regret would rouse them, and give birth to prayer,
Prayer would add faith, and faith would fix them there.
   Not that the Former of us all in this,
Or aught he does, is govern'd by caprice;
The supposition is replete with sin,
And bears the brand of blasphemy burnt in.
Not so—the silver trumpet's heavenly call
Sounds for the poor, but sounds alike for all:
Kings are invited, and would kings obey,
No slaves on earth more welcome were than they;
But royalty, nobility, and state,
Are such a dead preponderating weight,
That endless bliss, (how strange soe'er it seem,)
In counterpoise, flies up and kicks the beam.
'Tis open, and ye cannot enter—why?
Because ye will not, Conyers would reply—
And he says much that many may dispute
And cavil at with ease, but none refute.
Oh, bless'd effect of penury and want,
The seed sown there, how vigorous is the plant!
No soil like poverty for growth divine,
As leanest land supplies the richest wine.
Earth gives too little, giving only bread,
To nourish pride, or turn the weakest head:
To them the sounding jargon of the schools
Seems what it is—a cap and bells for fools:
The light they walk by, kindled from above,
Shows them the shortest way to life and love:
They, strangers to the controversial field,
Where deists, always foil'd, yet scorn to yield,
And never check'd by what impedes the wise,
Believe, rush forward, and possess the prize.
   Envy, ye great, the dull unletter'd small:
Ye have much cause for envy—but not all.

We boast some rich ones whom the Gospel sways,
And one who wears a coronet and prays;
Like gleanings of an olive tree, they show
Here and there one upon the topmost bough.
  How readily, upon the Gospel plan,
That question has its answer—What is man?
Sinful and weak, in every sense a wretch;
An instrument, whose chords, upon the stretch,
And strain'd to the last screw that he can bear,
Yield only discord in his Maker's ear:
Once the blest residence of truth divine,
Glorious as Solyma's interior shrine,
Where, in his own oracular abode,
Dwelt visibly the light-creating God;
But made long since, like Babylon of old,
A den of mischiefs never to be told:
And she, once mistress of the realms around,
Now scattered wide and no where to be found,
As soon shall rise and re-ascend the throne,
By native power and energy her own,
As nature, at her own peculiar cost,
Restore to man the glories he has lost.
Go—bid the winter cease to chill the year,
Replace the wandering comet in his sphere,
Then boast (but wait for that unhoped for hour)
The self-restoring arm of human power.
But what is man in his own proud esteem?
Hear him—himself the poet and the theme:
A monarch clothed with majesty and awe,
His mind his kingdom, and his will his law;
Grace in his mien, and glory in his eyes,
Supreme on earth, and worthy of the skies,
Strength in his heart, dominion in his nod,
And, thunderbolts excepted, quite a God!
  So sings he, charm'd with his own mind and form,
The song magnificent—the theme a worm!
Himself so much the source of his delight,
His Maker has no beauty in his sight.
See where he sits, contemplative and fix'd,
Pleasure and wonder in his features mix'd,
His passions tamed and all at his control,
How perfect the composure of his soul!
Complacency has breathed a gentle gale
O'er all his thoughts, and swell'd his easy sail:
His books well trimm'd, and in the gayest style,
Like regimental coxcombs, rank and file,
Adorn his intellects as well as shelves,
And teach him notions splendid as themselves:

The Bible only stands neglected there,
Though that of all most worthy of his care;
And, like an infant troublesome awake,
Is left to sleep for peace and quiet sake.
  What shall the man deserve of human kind,
Whose happy skill and industry combined
Shall prove (what argument could never yet)
The Bible an imposture and a cheat?
The praises of the libertine profess'd,
The worst of men, and curses of the best.
Where should the living, weeping o'er his woes;
The dying, trembling at the awful close;
Where the betray'd, forsaken, and oppress'd;
The thousands whom the world forbids to rest;
Where should they find, (those comforts at an end,
The Scripture yields,) or hope to find, a friend?
Sorrow might muse herself to madness then,
And, seeking exile from the sight of men,
Bury herself in solitude profound,
Grow frantic with her pangs, and bite the ground.
Thus often Unbelief, grown sick of life,
Flies to the tempting pool, or felon knife.
The jury meet, the coroner is short,
And lunacy the verdict of the court.
Reverse the sentence, let the truth be known,
Such lunacy is ignorance alone;
They knew not, what some bishops may not know,
That Scripture is the only cure of woe.
That field of promise how it flings abroad
Its odour o'er the Christian's thorny road!
The soul, reposing on assured relief,
Feels herself happy amidst all her grief,
Forgets her labour as she toils along,
Weeps tears of joy, and bursts into a song.
  But the same word, that, like the polish'd share,
Ploughs up the roots of a believer's care,
Kills too the flowery weeds, where'er they grow,
That bind the sinner's Bacchanalian brow.
Oh, that unwelcome voice of heavenly love,
Sad messenger of mercy from above!
How does it grate upon his thankless ear,
Crippling his pleasures with the cramp of fear!
His will and judgment at continual strife,
That civil war embitters all his life;
In vain he points his powers against the skies,
In vain he closes or averts his eyes,
Truth will intrude—she bids him yet beware;
And shakes the sceptic in the scorner's chair.

Though various foes against the Truth combine,
Pride above all opposes her design;
Pride, of a growth superior to the rest,
The subtlest serpent with the loftiest crest,
Swells at the thought, and, kindling into rage,
Would hiss the cherub Mercy from the stage.
   And is the soul indeed so lost?—she cries,
Fallen from her glory, and too weak to rise?
Torpid and dull, beneath a frozen zone,
Has she no spark that may be deem'd her own?
Grant her indebted to what zealots call
Grace undeserved, yet surely not for all!
Some beams of rectitude she yet displays,
Some love of virtue, and some power to praise;
Can lift herself above corporeal things,
And, soaring on her own unborrow'd wings,
Possess herself of all that's good or true,
Assert the skies, and vindicate her due.
Past indiscretion is a venial crime;
And if the youth, unmellowed yet by time,
Bore on his branch, luxuriant then and rude,
Fruits of a blighted size, austere and crude,
Maturer years shall happier stores produce,
And meliorate the well-concocted juice.
Then, conscious of her meritorious zeal,
To Justice she may make her bold appeal;
And leave to Mercy, with a tranquil mind,
The worthless and unfruitful of mankind.
Hear then how Mercy, slighted and defied,
Retorts the affront against the crown of pride.
   Perish the virtue, as it ought, abhorr'd,
And the fool with it, who insults his Lord.
The atonement a Redeemer's love has wrought
Is not for you—the righteous need it not.
Seest thou yon harlot, wooing all she meets,
The worn-out nuisance of the public streets,
Herself from morn to night, from night to morn,
Her own abhorrence, and as much your scorn?
The gracious shower, unlimited and free,
Shall fall on her, when Heaven denies it thee.
Of all that wisdom dictates, this the drift—
That man is dead in sin, and life a gift.
   Is virtue, then, unless of Christian growth,
Mere fallacy, or foolishness, or both?
Ten thousand sages lost in endless woe,
For ignorance of what they could not know?—
That speech betrays at once a bigot's tongue,
Charge not a God with such outrageous wrong!

Truly, not I—the partial light men have,
My creed persuades me, well employ'd, may save;
While he that scorns the noon-day beam, perverse,
Shall find the blessing, unimproved, a curse.
Let heathen worthies, whose exalted mind
Left sensuality and dross behind,
Possess, for me, their undisputed lot,
And take, unenvied, the reward they sought.
But still in virtue of a Saviour's plea,
Not blind by choice, but destined not to see.
Their fortitude and wisdom were a flame
Celestial, though they knew not whence it came,
Derived from the same source of light and grace,
That guides the Christian in his swifter race;
Their judge was conscience, and her rule their law:
That rule, pursued with reverence and with awe,
Led them, however faltering, faint, and slow,
From what they knew to what they wish'd to know.
But let not him that shares a brighter day
Traduce the splendour of a noontide ray,
Prefer the twilight of a darker time,
And deem his base stupidity no crime;
The wretch, who slights the bounty of the skies,
And sinks, while favour'd with the means to rise,
Shall find them rated at their full amount,
The good he scorn'd all carried to account.
    Marshalling all his terrors as he came,
Thunder, and earthquake, and devouring flame,
From Sinai's top Jehovah gave the law—
Life for obedience—death for every flaw.
When the great Sovereign would his will express,
He gives a perfect rule, what can he less?
And guards it with a sanction as severe
As vengeance can inflict, or sinners fear:
Else his own glorious rights he would disclaim,
And man might safely trifle with his name.
He bids him glow with unremitting love
To all on earth, and to himself above;
Condemns the injurious deed, the slanderous tongue,
The thought that meditates a brother's wrong:
Brings not alone the more conspicuous part,
His conduct, to the test, but tries his heart.
    Hark! universal nature shook and groan'd,
'Twas the last trumpet—see the Judge enthroned:
Rouse all your courage at your utmost need,
Now summon every virtue, stand and plead.
What! silent? Is your boasting heard no more?
That self-renouncing wisdom, learn'd before,

Had shed immortal glories on your brow,
That all your virtues cannot purchase now.
  All joy to the believer! He can speak—
Trembling yet happy, confident yet meek.
  Since the dear hour that brought me to thy foot
And cut up all my follies by the root,
I never trusted in an arm but thine,
Nor hoped, but in thy righteousness divine:
My prayers and alms, imperfect and defiled,
Were but the feeble efforts of a child;
Howe'er performed, it was their brightest part,
That they proceeded from a grateful heart:
Cleansed in thine own all-purifying blood,
Forgive their evil and accept their good:
I cast them at thy feet—my only plea
Is what it was, dependence upon thee:
While struggling in the vale of tears below,
That never fail'd, nor shall it fail me now.
  Angelic gratulations rend the skies,
Pride falls unpitied, never more to rise,
Humility is crown'd, and Faith receives the prize.

EXPOSTULATION

Tantane, tam patiens, nullo certamine tolli
Dona sines?
Virg.

THE ARGUMENT

Expostulation with the Muse weeping for England—Her apparently prosperous condition—State of Israel when the prophet wept over it—The Babylonian Captivity—When nations decline, the evil commences in the Church—State of the Jews in the time of our Saviour—Evidences of their having been the most favoured of nations—Causes of their downfall—Lesson taught by it—Warning to Britain—The hand of Providence to be traced in adverse events—England's transgressions—Her vain-glory—Her conduct towards India—Abuse of the sacrament—Obduracy against repentance—Futility of fasts—Character of the Clergy—The poet adverts to the state of the ancient Britons—Beneficial influence of the Roman power—England under papal supremacy—Favours since bestowed on her by Providence—Reasons for gratitude to God and for seeking to secure his favour—With that she may defy a world in arms—The poet anticipates little effect from his warning.

Why weeps the muse for England? What appears
In England's case to move the muse to tears?
From side to side of her delightful isle
Is she not clothed with a perpetual smile?

Can Nature add a charm, or Art confer
A new-found luxury, not seen in her?
Where under heaven is pleasure more pursued,
Or where does cold reflection less intrude?

Her fields a rich expanse of wavy corn,
Pour'd out from Plenty's overflowing horn;
Ambrosial gardens, in which art supplies
The fervour and the force of Indian skies;
Her peaceful shores, where busy Commerce waits
To pour his golden tide through all her gates;
Whom fiery suns, that scorch the russet spice
Of eastern groves, and oceans floor'd with ice,
Forbid in vain to push his daring way
To darker climes, or climes of brighter day;
Whom the winds waft where'er the billows roll,
From the World's girdle to the frozen pole;
The chariots bounding in her wheel-worn streets,
Her vaults below, where every vintage meets;
Her theatres, her revels, and her sports;
The scenes to which not youth alone resorts,
But age, in spite of weakness and of pain,
Still haunts, in hope to dream of youth again;
All speak her happy: let the muse look round
From East to West, no sorrow can be found;
Or only what, in cottages confined,
Sighs unregarded to the passing wind.
Then wherefore weep for England? What appears
In England's case to move the muse to tears?
   The prophet wept for Israel; wish'd his eyes
Were fountains fed with infinite supplies;
For Israel dealt in robbery and wrong;
There were the scorner's and the slanderer's tongue;
Oaths, used as playthings or convenient tools,
As interest biass'd knaves, or fashion fools;
Adultery, neighing at his neighbour's door;
Oppression labouring hard to grind the poor;
The partial balance and deceitful weight;
The treacherous smile, a mask for secret hate;
Hypocrisy, formality in prayer,
And the dull service of the lip were there.
Her women, insolent and self-caress'd,
By Vanity's unwearied finger dress'd,
Forgot the blush that virgin fears impart
To modest cheeks, and borrow'd one from art;
Were just such trifles, without worth or use,
As silly pride and idleness produce;
Curl'd, scented, furbelow'd, and flounced around,

With feet too delicate to touch the ground,
They stretch'd the neck, and roll'd the wanton eye,
And sigh'd for every fool that flutter'd by.
  He saw his people slaves to every lust,
Lewd, avaricious, arrogant, unjust;
He heard the wheels of an avenging God
Groan heavily along the distant road;
Saw Babylon set wide her two-leaved brass
To let the military deluge pass;
Jerusalem a prey, her glory soil'd,
Her princes captive, and her treasures spoil'd;
Wept till all Israel heard his bitter cry,
Stamp'd with his foot, and smote upon his thigh;
But wept, and stamp'd, and smote his thigh in vain,
Pleasure is deaf when told of future pain,
And sounds prophetic are too rough to suit
Ears long accustom'd to the pleasing lute:
They scorn'd his inspiration and his theme,
Pronounc'd him frantic, and his fears a dream;
With self-indulgence wing'd the fleeting hours,
Till the foe found them, and down fell the towers.
  Long time Assyria bound them in her chain,
Till penitence had purged the public stain,
And Cyrus, with relenting pity moved,
Return'd them happy to the land they loved;
There, proof against prosperity, awhile
They stood the test of her ensnaring smile,
And had the grace in scenes of peace to show
The virtue they had learn'd in scenes of woe.
But man is frail, and can but ill sustain
A long immunity from grief and pain;
And, after all the joys that Plenty leads,
With tiptoe step Vice silently succeeds.
  When he that ruled them with a shepherd's rod,
In form a man, in dignity a God,
Came, not expected in that humble guise,
To sift and search them with unerring eyes,
He found, conceal'd beneath a fair outside,
The filth of rottenness and worm of pride;
Their piety a system of deceit,
Scripture employ'd to sanctify the cheat;
The Pharisee the dupe of his own art,
Self-idolized, and yet a knave at heart.
  When nations are to perish in their sins,
'Tis in the church the leprosy begins;
The priest, whose office is, with zeal sincere,
To watch the fountain and preserve it clear,
Carelessly nods and sleeps upon the brink,

While others poison what the flock must drink;
Or, waking at the call of lust alone,
Infuses lies and errors of his own:
His unsuspecting sheep believe it pure;
And, tainted by the very means of cure,
Catch from each other a contagious spot,
The foul forerunner of a general rot.
Then truth is hush'd, that Heresy may preach;
And all is trash that reason cannot reach;
Then God's own image on the soul impress'd
Becomes a mockery and a standing jest;
And faith, the root whence only can arise
The graces of a life that wins the skies,
Loses at once all value and esteem,
Pronounced by graybeards a pernicious dream:
Then Ceremony leads her bigots forth,
Prepared to fight for shadows of no worth;
While truths, on which eternal things depend,
Find not, or hardly find, a single friend:
As soldiers watch the signal of command,
They learn to bow, to kneel, to sit, to stand;
Happy to fill religion's vacant place;
With hollow form, and gesture, and grimace.
  Such, when the Teacher of his church was there,
People and priest, the sons of Israel were;
Stiff in the letter, lax in the design
And import of their oracles divine;
Their learning legendary, false, absurd,
And yet exalted above God's own word;
They drew a curse from an intended good,
Puff'd up with gifts they never understood.
He judged them with as terrible a frown,
As if not love, but wrath, had brought him down:
Yet he was gentle as soft summer airs,
Had grace for others' sins, but none for theirs;
Through all he spoke a noble plainness ran—
Rhetoric is artifice, the work of man;
And tricks and turns, that fancy may devise,
Are far too mean for Him that rules the skies.
The astonish'd vulgar trembled while he tore
The mask from faces never seen before;
He stripp'd the impostors in the noonday sun,
Show'd that they follow'd all they seem'd to shun;
Their prayers made public, their excesses kept
As private as the chambers where they slept;
The temple and its holy rites profaned
By mummeries He that dwelt in it disdain'd;
Uplifted hands, that at convenient times

Could act extortion and the worst of crimes,
Wash'd with a neatness scrupulously nice,
And free from every taint but that of vice.
Judgment, however tardy, mends her pace
When obstinacy once has conquer'd grace.
They saw distemper heal'd, and life restored,
In answer to the fiat of his word;
Confess'd the wonder, and with daring tongue
Blasphemed the authority from which it sprung.
They knew, by sure prognostics seen on high,
The future tone and temper of the sky;
But, grave dissemblers! could not understand
That sin let loose speaks punishment at hand.
    Ask now of history's authentic page,
And call up evidence from every age;
Display with busy and laborious hand
The blessings of the most indebted land;
What nation will you find, whose annals prove
So rich an interest in Almighty love?
Where dwell they now, where dwelt in ancient day
A people planted, water'd, blest, as they?
Let Egypt's plagues and Canaan's woes proclaim
The favours pour'd upon the Jewish name;
Their freedom purchased for them at the cost
Of all their hard oppressors valued most:
Their title to a country not their own
Made sure by prodigies till then unknown;
For them the states they left made waste and void;
For them the states to which they went destroy'd;
A cloud to measure out their march by day,
By night a fire to cheer the gloomy way;
That moving signal summoning, when best,
Their host to move, and, when it stay'd, to rest.
For them the rocks dissolved into a flood,
The dews condensed into angelic food,
Their very garments sacred, old yet new,
And Time forbid to touch them as he flew;
Streams, swell'd above the bank, enjoin'd to stand
While they pass'd through to their appointed land;
Their leader arm'd with meekness, zeal, and love,
And graced with clear credentials from above;
Themselves secured beneath the Almighty wing;
Their God their captain, lawgiver, and king;
Crown'd with a thousand victories, and at last
Lords of the conquer'd soil, there rooted fast,
In peace possessing what they won by war,
Their name far publish'd, and revered as far;
Where will you find a race like theirs, endow'd

With all that man e'er wish'd, or Heaven bestow'd?
 They, and they only, amongst all mankind,
Received the transcript of the Eternal Mind:
Were trusted with his own engraven laws,
And constituted guardians of his cause;
Theirs were the prophets, theirs the priestly call,
And theirs by birth the Saviour of us all.
In vain the nations, that had seen them rise
With fierce and envious, yet admiring, eyes,
Had sought to crush them, guarded as they were
By power divine and skill that could not err.
Had they maintain'd allegiance firm and sure,
And kept the faith immaculate and pure,
Then the proud eagles of all-conquering Rome
Had found one city not to be o'ercome;
And the twelve standards of the tribes unfurl'd
Had bid defiance to the warring world.
But grace abused brings forth the foulest deeds,
As richest soil the most luxuriant weeds.
Cured of the golden calves, their fathers' sin,
They set up self, that idol god within;
View'd a Deliverer with disdain and hate,
Who left them still a tributary state;
Seized fast his hand, held out to set them free
From a worse yoke, and nail'd it to the tree:
There was the consummation and the crown,
The flower of Israel's infamy full blown;
Thence date their sad declension, and their fall,
Their woes, not yet repeal'd, thence date them all.
 Thus fell the best instructed in her day,
And the most favour'd land, look where we may.
Philosophy indeed on Grecian eyes
Had pour'd the day, and clear'd the Roman skies;
In other climes perhaps creative art,
With power surpassing theirs, performed her part;
Might give more life to marble, or might fill
The glowing tablets with a juster skill,
Might shine in fable, and grace idle themes
With all the embroidery of poetic dreams;
'Twas theirs alone to dive into the plan
That truth and mercy had reveal'd to man;
And, while the world beside, that plan unknown,
Deified useless wood or senseless stone,
They breathed in faith their well-directed prayers,
And the true God, the God of truth, was theirs.
 Their glory faded, and their race dispersed,
The last of nations now, though once the first,
They warn and teach the proudest, would they learn

Keep wisdom, or meet vengeance in your turn:
If we escaped not, if Heaven spared not us,
Peel'd, scatter'd, and exterminated thus;
If vice received her retribution due,
When we were visited, what hope for you?
When God arises with an awful frown,
To punish lust, or pluck presumption down;
When gifts perverted, or not duly prized,
Pleasure o'ervalued, and his grace despised,
Provoke the vengeance of his righteous hand,
To pour down wrath upon a thankless land:
He will be found impartially severe,
Too just to wink, or speak the guilty clear.
   Oh Israel, of all nations most undone!
Thy diadem displaced, thy sceptre gone;
Thy temple, once thy glory, fallen and rased,
And thou a worshipper e'en where thou mayst;
Thy services, once holy without spot,
Mere shadows now, their ancient pomp forgot;
Thy Levites, once a consecrated host,
No longer Levites, and their lineage lost,
And thou thyself o'er every country sown,
With none on earth that thou canst call thine own;
Cry aloud, thou that sittest in the dust,
Cry to the proud, the cruel, and unjust;
Knock at the gates of nations, rouse their fears;
Say wrath is coming, and the storm appears;
But raise the shrillest cry in British ears.
   What ails thee, restless as the waves that roar,
And fling their foam against thy chalky shore?
Mistress, at least while Providence shall please,
And trident-bearing queen of the wide seas—
Why, having kept good faith, and often shown
Friendship and truth to others, find'st thou none?
Thou that hast set the persecuted free,
None interposes now to succour thee.
Countries indebted to thy power, that shine
With light derived from thee, would smother thine.
Thy very children watch for thy disgrace,
A lawless brood, and curse thee to thy face.
Thy rulers load thy credit, year by year,
With sums Peruvian mines could never clear;
As if, like arches built with skilful hand,
The more 'twere press'd the firmer it would stand.
   The cry in all thy ships is still the same,
Speed us away to battle and to fame.
Thy mariners explore the wild expanse,
Impatient to descry the flags of France:

But, though they fight as thine have ever fought,
Return ashamed without the wreaths they sought.
Thy senate is a scene of civil jar,
Chaos of contrarieties at war;
Where sharp and solid, phlegmatic and light,
Discordant atoms meet, ferment, and fight;
Where obstinacy takes his sturdy stand,
To disconcert what policy has plann'd;
Where policy is busied all night long
In setting right what faction has set wrong;
Where flails of oratory thresh the floor,
That yields them chaff and dust, and nothing more.
Thy rack'd inhabitants repine, complain,
Tax'd till the brow of labour sweats in vain;
War lays a burden on the reeling state,
And peace does nothing to relieve the weight;
Successive loads succeeding broils impose,
And sighing millions prophesy the close.
  Is adverse Providence, when ponder'd well,
So dimly writ, or difficult to spell,
Thou canst not read with readiness and ease
Providence adverse in events like these?
Know then that heavenly wisdom on this ball
Creates, gives birth to, guides, consummates all;
That, while laborious and quick-thoughted man
Snuffs up the praise of what he seems to plan,
He first conceives, then perfects his design,
As a mere instrument in hands divine:
Blind to the working of that secret power
That balances the wings of every hour,
The busy trifler dreams himself alone,
Frames many a purpose, and God works his own.
States thrive or wither as moons wax and wane,
E'en as his will and his decrees ordain;
While honour, virtue, piety, bear sway,
They flourish; and, as these decline, decay:
In just resentment of his injured laws,
He pours contempt on them and on their cause;
Strikes the rough thread of error right athwart
The web of every scheme they have at heart;
Bids rottenness invade and bring to dust
The pillars of support, in which they trust,
And do his errand of disgrace and shame
On the chief strength and glory of the frame.
None ever yet impeded what he wrought,
None bars him out from his most secret thought;
Darkness itself before his eye is light,
And hell's close mischief naked in his sight.

Stand now and judge thyself—Hast thou incurr'd
His anger who can waste thee with a word,
Who poises and proportions sea and land,
Weighing them in the hollow of his hand,
And in whose awful sight all nations seem
As grasshoppers, as dust, a drop, a dream?
Hast thou (a sacrilege his soul abhors)
Claim'd all the glory of thy prosperous wars?
Proud of thy fleets and armies, stolen the gem
Of his just praise, to lavish it on them?
Hast thou not learn'd, what thou art often told,
A truth still sacred, and believed of old,
That no success attends on spears and swords
Unblest, and that the battle is the Lord's?
That courage is his creature; and dismay
The post, that at his bidding speeds away,
Ghastly in feature, and his stammering tongue
With doleful humour and sad presage hung,
To quell the valour of the stoutest heart,
And teach the combatant a woman's part?
That he bids thousands fly when none pursue,
Saves as he will by many or by few,
And claims for ever, as his royal right,
The event and sure decision of the fight?
  Hast thou, though suckled at fair freedom's breast,
Exported slavery to the conquer'd East?
Pull'd down the tyrants India served with dread,
And raised thyself, a greater, in their stead?
Gone thither arm'd and hungry, return'd full,
Fed from the richest veins of the Mogul,
A despot big with power obtain'd by wealth,
And that obtain'd by rapine and by stealth?
With Asiatic vices stored thy mind,
But left their virtues and thine own behind?
And, having truck'd thy soul, brought home the fee,
To tempt the poor to sell himself to thee?
  Hast thou by statute shoved from its design,
The Saviour's feast, his own blest bread and wine,
And made the symbols of atoning grace
An office-key, a picklock to a place,
That infidels may prove their title good
By an oath dipp'd in sacramental blood?
A blot that will be still a blot, in spite
Of all that grave apologists may write;
And though a bishop toil to cleanse the stain,
He wipes and scours the silver cup in vain.
And hast thou sworn on every slight pretence,
Till perjuries are common as bad pence,

While thousands, careless of the damning sin
Kiss the book's outside, who ne'er look within?
   Hast thou, when Heaven has clothed thee with disgrace,
And, long provoked, repaid thee to thy face,
(For thou hast known eclipses, and endured
Dimness and anguish, all thy beams obscured,
When sin has shed dishonour on thy brow;
And never of a sabler hue than now,)
Hast thou, with heart perverse and conscience sear'd,
Despising all rebuke, still persevered,
And, having chosen evil, scorn'd the voice
That cried, Repent!—and gloried in thy choice?
Thy fastings, when calamity at last
Suggests the expedient of a yearly fast,
What mean they? Canst thou dream there is a power
In lighter diet at a later hour,
To charm to sleep the threatening of the skies,
And hide past folly from all-seeing eyes?
The fast that wins deliverance, and suspends
The stroke that a vindictive God intends,
Is to renounce hypocrisy; to draw
Thy life upon the pattern of the law;
To war with pleasure, idolized before;
To vanquish lust, and wear its yoke no more.
All fasting else, whate'er be the pretence,
Is wooing mercy by renew'd offence.
   Hast thou within thee sin, that in old time
Brought fire from heaven, the sex-abusing crime,
Whose horrid perpetration stamps disgrace,
Baboons are free from, upon human race?
Think on the fruitful and well-water'd spot
That fed the flocks and herds of wealthy Lot,
Where Paradise seem'd still vouchsafed on earth,
Burning and scorch'd into perpetual dearth,
Or, in his words who damn'd the base desire,
Suffering the vengeance of eternal fire:
Then nature, injured, scandalized, defiled,
Unveil'd her blushing cheek, look'd on, and smiled;
Beheld with joy the lovely scene defac'd,
And praised the wrath that laid her beauties waste.
   Far be the thought from any verse of mine,
And farther still the form'd and fix'd design,
To thrust the charge of deeds that I detest
Against an innocent unconscious breast;
The man that dares traduce, because he can
With safety to himself, is not a man:
An individual is a sacred mark,
Not to be pierced in play, or in the dark;

But public censure speaks a public foe,
Unless a zeal for virtue guide the blow.
   The priestly brotherhood, devout, sincere,
From mean self-interest, and ambition clear,
Their hope in heaven, servility their scorn,
Prompt to persuade, expostulate, and warn,
Their wisdom pure, and given them from above,
Their usefulness ensured by zeal and love,
As meek as the man Moses, and withal
As bold as in Agrippa's presence Paul,
Should fly the world's contaminating touch,
Holy and unpolluted:—are thine such?
Except a few with Eli's spirit blest,
Hophni and Phineas may describe the rest.
   Where shall a teacher look, in days like these,
For ears and hearts that he can hope to please?
Look to the poor—the simple and the plain
Will hear perhaps thy salutary strain:
Humility is gentle, apt to learn,
Speak but the word, will listen and return.
Alas, not so! the poorest of the flock
Are proud, and set their faces as a rock;
Denied that earthly opulence they choose,
God's better gift they scoff at and refuse.
The rich, the produce of a nobler stem,
Are more intelligent, at least—try them.
Oh vain inquiry! they without remorse
Are altogether gone a devious course;
Where beckoning pleasure leads them, wildly stray;
Have burst the bands, and cast the yoke away.
   Now borne upon the wings of truth sublime,
Review thy dim original and prime.
This island, spot of unreclaim'd rude earth,
The cradle that received thee at thy birth,
Was rock'd by many a rough Norwegian blast,
And Danish howlings scared thee as they pass'd;
For thou wast born amid the din of arms,
And suck'd a breast that panted with alarms.
While yet thou wast a grovelling, puling chit,
Thy bones not fashion'd, and thy joints not knit,
The Roman taught thy stubborn knee to bow,
Though twice a Cæsar could not bend thee now.
His victory was that of orient light,
When the sun's shafts disperse the gloom of night.
Thy language at this distant moment shows
How much the country to the conqueror owes;
Expressive, energetic, and refined,
It sparkles with the gems he left behind;

He brought thy land a blessing when he came,
He found thee savage, and he left thee tame;
Taught thee to clothe thy pink'd and painted hide,
And grac'd thy figure with a soldier's pride;
He sow'd the seeds of order where he went,
Improv'd thee far beyond his own intent,
And, while he ruled thee by the sword alone,
Made thee at last a warrior like his own.
Religion, if in heavenly truths attired,
Needs only to be seen to be admired;
But thine, as dark as witcheries of the night,
Was form'd to harden hearts and shock the sight;
Thy druids struck the well-hung harps they bore
With fingers deeply dyed in human gore;
And while the victim slowly bled to death,
Upon the rolling chords rung out his dying breath.
  Who brought the lamp that with awaking beams
Dispell'd thy gloom, and broke away thy dreams,
Tradition, now decrepit and worn out,
Babbler of ancient fables, leaves a doubt:
But still light reach'd thee; and those gods of thine,
Woden and Thor, each tottering in his shrine,
Fell broken and defaced at their own door,
As Dagon in Philistia long before.
But Rome with sorceries and magic wand
Soon raised a cloud that darken'd every land;
And thine was smother'd in the stench and fog
Of Tiber's marshes and the papal bog.
Then priests with bulls and briefs, and shaven crowns,
And griping fists, and unrelenting frowns,
Legates and delegates with powers from hell,
Though heavenly in pretension, fleeced thee well;
And to this hour, to keep it fresh in mind,
Some twigs of that old scourge are left behind.
Thy soldiery, the pope's well managed pack,
Were train'd beneath his lash, and knew the smack,
And, when he laid them on the scent of blood,
Would hunt a Saracen through fire and flood.
Lavish of life, to win an empty tomb,
That proved a mint of wealth, a mine to Rome,
They left their bones beneath unfriendly skies,
His worthless absolution all the prize.
Thou wast the veriest slave, in days of yore
That ever dragg'd a chain or tugg'd an oar;
Thy monarchs arbitrary, fierce, unjust,
Themselves the slaves of bigotry or lust,
Disdain'd thy counsels, only in distress
Found thee a goodly spunge for power to press.

Thy chiefs, the lords of many a petty fee,
Provoked and harass'd, in return plagued thee;
Call'd thee away from peaceable employ,
Domestic happiness and rural joy,
To waste thy life in arms, or lay it down
In causeless feuds and bickerings of their own.
Thy parliaments adored, on bended knees,
The sovereignty they were convened to please;
Whate'er was ask'd, too timid to resist,
Complied with, and were graciously dismiss'd;
And if some Spartan soul a doubt express'd,
And, blushing at the tameness of the rest,
Dared to suppose the subject had a choice,
He was a traitor by the general voice.
Oh slave! with powers thou didst not dare exert,
Verse cannot stoop so low as thy desert;
It shakes the sides of splenetic disdain,
Thou self-entitled ruler of the main,
To trace thee to the date, when yon fair sea,
That clips thy shores, had no such charms for thee;
When other nations flew from coast to coast,
And thou hadst neither fleet nor flag to boast.
Kneel now, and lay thy forehead in the dust;
Blush if thou canst; not petrified, thou must;
Act but an honest and a faithful part;
Compare what then thou wast with what thou art;
And God's disposing providence confess'd,
Obduracy itself must yield the rest.—
Then thou art bound to serve him, and to prove,
Hour after hour, thy gratitude and love.

   Has he not hid thee and thy favour'd land,
For ages, safe beneath his sheltering hand,
Given thee his blessing on the clearest proof,
Bid nations leagued against thee stand aloof,
And charged hostility and hate to roar
Where else they would, but not upon thy shore?
His power secured thee, when presumptuous Spain
Baptized her fleet invincible in vain;
Her gloomy monarch, doubtful and resign'd
To every pang that racks an anxious mind,
Ask'd of the waves that broke upon his coast,
What tidings? and the surge replied—All lost!
And when the Stuart, leaning on the Scot,
Then too much fear'd, and now too much forgot,
Pierced to the very centre of the realm,
And hoped to seize his abdicated helm,
'Twas but to prove how quickly, with a frown,
He that had raised thee could have pluck'd thee down.

Peculiar is the grace by thee possess'd,
Thy foes implacable, thy land at rest;
Thy thunders travel over earth and seas,
And all at home is pleasure, wealth, and ease.
'Tis thus, extending his tempestuous arm,
Thy Maker fills the nations with alarm,
While his own heaven surveys the troubled scene,
And feels no change, unshaken and serene.
Freedom, in other lands scarce known to shine,
Pours out a flood of splendour upon thine;
Thou hast as bright an interest in her rays
As ever Roman had in Rome's best days.
True freedom is where no restraint is known
That Scripture, justice, and good sense disown.
Where only vice and injury are tied,
And all from shore to shore is free beside.
Such freedom is—and Windsor's hoary towers
Stood trembling at the boldness of thy powers,
That won a nymph on that immortal plain,
Like her the fabled Phœbus wooed in vain:
He found the laurel only—happier you
The unfading laurel, and the virgin too!
   Now think, if pleasure have a thought to spare;
If God himself be not beneath her care;
If business, constant as the wheels of time,
Can pause an hour to read a serious rhyme;
If the new mail thy merchants now receive,
Or expectation of the next, give leave;
Oh think, if chargeable with deep arrears
For such indulgence gilding all thy years,
How much, though long neglected, shining yet,
The beams of heavenly truth have swell'd the debt.
When persecuting zeal made royal sport
With tortured innocence in Mary's court,
And Bonner, blithe as shepherd at a wake,
Enjoyed the show, and danced about the stake,
The sacred book, its value understood,
Received the seal of martyrdom in blood.
Those holy men, so full of truth and grace,
Seem to reflection of a different race,
Meek, modest, venerable, wise, sincere,
In such a cause they could not dare to fear;
They could not purchase earth with such a prize,
Or spare a life too short to reach the skies.
From them to thee conveyed along the tide,
Their streaming hearts pour'd freely when they died;
Those truths, which neither use nor years impair,
Invite thee, woo thee, to the bliss they share.

What dotage will not vanity maintain?
What web too weak to catch a modern brain?
The moles and bats in full assembly find,
On special search, the keen-eyed eagle blind.
And did they dream, and art thou wiser now?
Prove it—if better, I submit and bow.
Wisdom and goodness are twin-born, one heart
Must hold both sisters, never seen apart.
So then—as darkness overspread the deep,
Ere nature rose from her eternal sleep,
And this delightful earth, and that fair sky,
Leap'd out of nothing, call'd by the Most High;
By such a change thy darkness is made light,
Thy chaos order, and thy weakness might;
And He, whose power mere nullity obeys,
Who found thee nothing, form'd thee for his praise.
To praise him is to serve him, and fulfil,
Doing and suffering, his unquestioned will;
'Tis to believe what men inspired of old,
Faithful, and faithfully informed, unfold;
Candid and just, with no false aim in view,
To take for truth what cannot but be true;
To learn in God's own school the Christian part,
And bind the task assigned thee to thine heart:
Happy the man there seeking and there found;
Happy the nation where such men abound!
   How shall a verse impress thee? by what name
Shall I adjure thee not to court thy shame?
By theirs whose bright example, unimpeached,
Directs thee to that eminence they reached,
Heroes and worthies of days past, thy sires?
Or his, who touch'd their hearts with hallow'd fires?
Their names, alas! in vain reproach an age,
Whom all the vanities they scorn'd engage;
And his, that seraphs tremble at, is hung
Disgracefully on every trifler's tongue,
Or serves the champion in forensic war
To flourish and parade with at the bar.
Pleasure herself perhaps suggests a plea,
If interest move thee, to persuade e'en thee;
By every charm that smiles upon her face,
By joys possess'd, and joys still held in chase,
If dear society be worth a thought,
And if the feast of freedom cloy thee not,
Reflect that these, and all that seems thine own,
Held by the tenure of his will alone,
Like angels in the service of their Lord,
Remain with thee, or leave thee at his word;

That gratitude, and temperance in our use
Of what he gives, unsparing and profuse,
Secure the favour, and enhance the joy,
That thankless waste and wild abuse destroy.
But above all reflect, how cheap soe'er
Those rights, that millions envy thee, appear,
And though resolved to risk them, and swim down
The tide of pleasure, heedless of his frown,
That blessings truly sacred, and when given
Mark'd with the signature and stamp of Heaven,
The word of prophecy, those truths divine,
Which make that heaven, if thou desire it, thine,
(Awful alternative! believed, beloved,
Thy glory, and thy shame if unimproved,)
Are never long vouchsafed, if push'd aside
With cold disgust or philosophic pride;
And that, judicially withdrawn, disgrace,
Error, and darkness, occupy their place.
　　A world is up in arms, and thou, a spot
Not quickly found, if negligently sought,
Thy soul as ample as thy bounds are small,
Endur'st the brunt, and dar'st defy them all;
And wilt thou join to this bold enterprise
A bolder still, a contest with the skies?
Remember, if He guard thee and secure,
Whoe'er assails thee, thy success is sure;
But if He leave thee, though the skill and power
Of nations, sworn to spoil thee and devour,
Were all collected in thy single arm,
And thou couldst laugh away the fear of harm,
That strength would fail, opposed against the push
And feeble onset of a pigmy rush.
Say not (and if the thought of such defence
Should spring within thy bosom, drive it thence)
What nation amongst all my foes is free
From crimes as base as any charged on me?
Their measure fill'd, they too shall pay the debt,
Which God, though long forborne, will not forget.
But know that wrath divine, when most severe,
Makes justice still the guide of his career,
And will not punish, in one mingled crowd,
Them without light, and thee without a cloud.
　·　　Muse, hang this harp upon yon aged beech,
Still murmuring with the solemn truths I teach;
And, while at intervals a cold blast sings
Through the dry leaves, and pants upon the strings,
My soul shall sigh in secret, and lament
A nation scourged, yet tardy to repent.

I know the warning song is sung in vain;
That few will hear, and fewer heed the strain;
But if a sweeter voice, and one design'd
A blessing to my country and mankind,
Reclaim the wandering thousands, and bring home
A flock so scatter'd and so wont to roam,
Then place it once again between my knees;
The sound of truth will then be sure to please;
And truth alone, where'er my life be cast,
In scenes of plenty, or the pining waste,
Shall be my chosen theme, my glory to the last.

HOPE

..... doceas iter, et sacra ostia pandas.
Virg. Æn. 6.

THE ARGUMENT

Human Life—The charms of Nature remain the same though they appear different in youth and age—
Frivolity of fashionable life—Value of life—The works of the Creator evidences of his attributes—Nature
the handmaid to the purposes of grace—Character of Hope—Man naturally stubborn and intractable—
His conduct in different stations—Death's honours—Each man's belief right in his own eyes—Simile of
Ethelred's hospitality—Mankind quarrel with the Giver of eternal life, on account of the terms on which it
is offered—Opinions on this subject—Spread of the Gospel—The Greenland Missions—Contrast of the
unconverted and converted heathen—Character of Leuconomus—The man of pleasure the blindest of
bigots—Any hope preferred to that required by the Scripture—Human nature opposed to Truth—
Apostrophe to Truth—Picture of one conscience-smitten—The pardoned sinner—Conclusion.

Ask what is human life—the sage replies,
With disappointment lowering in his eyes,
A painful passage o'er a restless flood,
A vain pursuit of fugitive false good,
A scene of fancied bliss and heartfelt care,
Closing at last in darkness and despair.
The poor, inured to drudgery and distress,
Act without aim, think little, and feel less,
And no where, but in feign'd Arcadian scenes,
Taste happiness, or know what pleasure means.
Riches are pass'd away from hand to hand,
As fortune, vice, or folly may command;
As in a dance the pair that take the lead
Turn downward, and the lowest pair succeed,
So shifting and so various is the plan
By which Heaven rules the mix'd affairs of man;

Vicissitude wheels round the motley crowd,
The rich grow poor, the poor become purse-proud;
Business is labour, and man's weakness such,
Pleasure is labour too, and tires as much,
The very sense of it foregoes its use,
By repetition pall'd, by age obtuse.
Youth lost in dissipation, we deplore,
Through life's sad remnant, what no sighs restore;
Our years, a fruitless race without a prize,
Too many, yet too few to make us wise.

   Dangling his cane about, and taking snuff,
Lothario cries, What philosophic stuff—
O querulous and weak!—whose useless brain
Once thought of nothing, and now thinks in vain;
Whose eye reverted weeps o'er all the past,
Whose prospect shows thee a disheartening waste;
Would age in thee resign his wint'ry reign,
And youth invigorate that frame again,
Renew'd desire would grace with other speech
Joys always prized, when placed within our reach.

   For lift thy palsied head, shake off the gloom
That overhangs the borders of thy tomb,
See nature gay, as when she first began
With smiles alluring her admirer man;
She spreads the morning over eastern hills,
Earth glitters with the drops the night distils;
The sun, obedient, at her call appears
To fling his glories o'er the robe she wears;
Banks clothed with flowers, groves fill'd with sprightly sounds,
The yellow tilth, green meads, rocks, rising grounds,
Streams, edged with osiers, fattening every field
Where'er they flow, now seen and now conceal'd;
From the blue rim, where skies and mountains meet,
Down to the very turf beneath thy feet,
Ten thousand charms, that only fools despise,
Or pride can look at with indifferent eyes,
All speak one language, all with one sweet voice
Cry to her universal realm, Rejoice!
Man feels the spur of passions and desires,
And she gives largely more than he requires;
Not that, his hours devoted all to care,
Hollow-eyed abstinence, and lean despair,
The wretch may pine, while to his smell, taste, sight,
She holds a paradise of rich delight;
But gently to rebuke his awkward fear,
To prove that what she gives she gives sincere,
To banish hesitation, and proclaim
His happiness her dear, her only, aim.

'Tis grave philosophy's absurdest dream,
That Heaven's intentions are not what they seem,
That only shadows are dispensed below,
And earth has no reality but woe.
  Thus things terrestrial wear a different hue,
As youth or age persuades; and neither true.
So, Flora's wreath through colour'd crystal seen,
The rose or lily appears blue or green,
But still the imputed tints are those alone
The medium represents, and not their own.
  To rise at noon, sit slipshod and undress'd,
To read the news, or fiddle, as seems best,
Till half the world comes rattling at his door,
To fill the dull vacuity till four;
And, just when evening turns the blue vault gray,
To spend two hours in dressing for the day;
To make the sun a bauble without use,
Save for the fruits his heavenly beams produce;
Quite to forget, or deem it worth no thought,
Who bids him shine, or if he shine or not;
Through mere necessity to close his eyes
Just when the larks and when the shepherds rise;
Is such a life, so tediously the same,
So void of all utility or aim,
That poor Jonquil, with almost every breath,
Sighs for his exit, vulgarly called death:
For he, with all his follies, has a mind
Not yet so blank, or fashionably blind,
But now and then perhaps a feeble ray
Of distant wisdom shoots across his way;
By which he reads, that life without a plan,
As useless as the moment it began,
Serves merely as a soil for discontent
To thrive in; an incumbrance ere half spent.
Oh! weariness beyond what asses feel,
That tread the circuit of the cistern wheel;
A dull rotation, never at a stay,
Yesterday's face twin image of to-day;
While conversation, an exhausted stock,
Grows drowsy as the clicking of a clock.
No need, he cries, of gravity stuff'd out
With academic dignity devout,
To read wise lectures, vanity the text:
Proclaim the remedy, ye learned, next;
For truth self-evident, with pomp impress'd,
Is vanity surpassing all the rest.
  That remedy, not hid in deeps profound,
Yet seldom sought where only to be found,

While passion turns aside from its due scope
The inquirer's aim, that remedy is Hope.
Life is his gift, from whom whate'er life needs,
With every good and perfect gift, proceeds;
Bestow'd on man, like all that we partake,
Royally, freely, for his bounty's sake;
Transient indeed, as is the fleeting hour,
And yet the seed of an immortal flower;
Design'd, in honour of his endless love,
To fill with fragrance his abode above;
No trifle, howsoever short it seem,
And, howsoever shadowy, no dream;
Its value, what no thought can ascertain,
Nor all an angel's eloquence explain.
Men deal with life as children with their play,
Who first misuse, then cast their toys away;
Live to no sober purpose, and contend
That their Creator had no serious end.
When God and man stand opposite in view,
Man's disappointment must, of course, ensue.
The just Creator condescends to write,
In beams of inextinguishable light,
His names of wisdom, goodness, power, and love,
On all that blooms below, or shines above;
To catch the wandering notice of mankind,
And teach the world, if not perversely blind,
His gracious attributes, and prove the share
His offspring hold in his paternal care.
If, led from earthly things to things divine,
His creature thwart not his august design,
Then praise is heard instead of reasoning pride,
And captious cavil and complaint subside.
Nature, employ'd in her allotted place,
Is handmaid to the purposes of grace;
By good vouchsafed makes known superior good,
And bliss not seen by blessings understood:
That bliss, reveal'd in scripture, with a glow
Bright as the covenant-ensuring bow,
Fires all his feelings with a noble scorn
Of sensual evil, and thus Hope is born.
  Hope sets the stamp of vanity on all
That men have deem'd substantial since the fall,
Yet has the wondrous virtue to educe
From emptiness itself a real use;
And while she takes, as at a father's hand,
What health and sober appetite demand,
From fading good derives, with chemic art,
That lasting happiness, a thankful heart.

Hope, with uplifted foot, set free from earth,
Pants for the place of her ethereal birth,
On steady wings sails through the immense abyss,
Plucks amaranthine joys from bowers of bliss,
And crowns the soul, while yet a mourner here,
With wreaths like those triumphant spirits wear.
Hope, as an anchor, firm and sure, holds fast
The Christian vessel, and defies the blast.
Hope! nothing else can nourish and secure
His new-born virtues, and preserve him pure.
Hope! let the wretch, once conscious of the joy,
Whom now despairing agonies destroy,
Speak, for he can, and none so well as he,
What treasures centre, what delights, in thee.
Had he the gems, the spices, and the land,
That boasts the treasure, all at his command;
The fragrant grove, the inestimable mine,
Were light, when weigh'd against one smile of thine.
    Though clasp'd and cradled in his nurse's arms,
He shines with all a cherub's artless charms,
Man is the genuine offspring of revolt,
Stubborn and sturdy, a wild ass's colt;
His passions, like the watery stores that sleep
Beneath the smiling surface of the deep,
Wait but the lashes of a wintry storm,
To frown and roar, and shake his feeble form.
From infancy through childhood's giddy maze,
Froward at school, and fretful in his plays,
The puny tyrant burns to subjugate
The free republic of the whip-gig state.
If one, his equal in athletic frame,
Or, more provoking still, of nobler name,
Dare step across his arbitrary views,
An Iliad, only not in verse, ensues:
The little Greeks look trembling at the scales,
Till the best tongue or heaviest hand prevails.
    Now see him launch'd into the world at large;
If priest, supinely droning o'er his charge,
Their fleece his pillow, and his weekly drawl,
Though short, too long, the price he pays for all.
If lawyer, loud whatever cause he plead,
But proudest of the worst, if that succeed.
Perhaps a grave physician, gathering fees,
Punctually paid for lengthening out disease;
No Cotton, whose humanity sheds rays,
That make superior skill his second praise.
If arms engage him, he devotes to sport
His date of life so likely to be short;

A soldier may be any thing, if brave,
So may a tradesman, if not quite a knave.
Such stuff the world is made of; and mankind
To passion, interest, pleasure, whim, resign'd,
Insist on, as if each were his own pope,
Forgiveness, and the privilege of hope;
But conscience, in some awful silent hour,
When captivating lusts have lost their power,
Perhaps when sickness, or some fearful dream,
Reminds him of religion, hated theme!
Starts from the down, on which she lately slept,
And tells of laws despised, at least not kept;
Shows with a pointing finger, but no noise,
A pale procession of past sinful joys,
All witnesses of blessings foully scorn'd,
And life abused, and not to be suborn'd.
Mark these, she says; these, summon'd from afar,
Begin their march to meet thee at the bar;
There find a Judge inexorably just,
And perish there, as all presumption must.
   Peace be to those (such peace as earth can give)
Who live in pleasure, dead e'en while they live;
Born capable indeed of heavenly truth;
But down to latest age, from earliest youth,
Their mind a wilderness through want of care,
The plough of wisdom never entering there.
Peace (if insensibility may claim
A right to the meek honours of her name)
To men of pedigree, their noble race,
Emulous always of the nearest place
To any throne, except the throne of grace.
Let cottagers and unenlighten'd swains
Revere the laws they dream that Heaven ordains;
Resort on Sundays to the house of prayer,
And ask, and fancy they find, blessings there.
Themselves, perhaps, when weary they retreat
To enjoy cool nature in a country seat,
To exchange the centre of a thousand trades,
For clumps, and lawns, and temples, and cascades,
May now and then their velvet cushions take,
And seem to pray for good example sake;
Judging, in charity no doubt, the town
Pious enough, and having need of none.
Kind souls! to teach their tenantry to prize
What they themselves, without remorse, despise:
Nor hope have they, nor fear, of aught to come,
As well for them had prophecy been dumb;
They could have held the conduct they pursue,

Had Paul of Tarsus lived and died a Jew;
And truth, proposed to reasoners wise as they,
Is a pearl cast—completely cast away,
   They die.—Death lends them, pleased, and as in sport,
All the grim honours of his ghastly court.
Far other paintings grace the chamber now,
Where late we saw the mimic landscape glow:
The busy heralds hang the sable scene
With mournful 'scutcheons, and dim lamps between;
Proclaim their titles to the crowd around,
But they that wore them move not at the sound;
The coronet, placed idly at their head,
Adds nothing now to the degraded dead,
And e'en the star, that glitters on the bier,
Can only say—Nobility lies here.
Peace to all such—'twere pity to offend,
By useless censure, whom we cannot mend;
Life without hope can close but in despair,
'Twas there we found them, and must leave them there.
   As when two pilgrims in a forest stray,
Both may be lost, yet each in his own way;
So fares it with the multitudes beguiled
In vain opinion's waste and dangerous wild;
Ten thousand rove the brakes and thorns among,
Some eastward, and some westward, and all wrong.
But here, alas! the fatal difference lies,
Each man's belief is right in his own eyes;
And he that blames what they have blindly chose
Incurs resentment for the love he shows.
   Say, botanist, within whose province fall
The cedar and the hyssop on the wall,
Of all that deck the lanes, the fields, the bowers,
What parts the kindred tribes of weeds and flowers?
Sweet scent, or lovely form, or both combined,
Distinguish every cultivated kind;
The want of both denotes a meaner breed,
And Chloe from her garland picks the weed.
Thus hopes of every sort, whatever sect
Esteem them, sow them, rear them, and protect,
If wild in nature, and not duly found,
Gethsemane! in thy dear hallow'd ground,
That cannot bear the blaze of Scripture light,
Nor cheer the spirit, nor refresh the sight,
Nor animate the soul to Christian deeds,
(Oh cast them from thee!) are weeds, arrant weeds.
   Ethelred's house, the centre of six ways,
Diverging each from each, like equal rays,
Himself as bountiful as April rains,

Lord paramount of the surrounding plains,
Would give relief of bed and board to none,
But guests that sought it in the appointed One;
And they might enter at his open door,
E'en till his spacious hall would hold no more.
He sent a servant forth by every road,
To sound his horn and publish it abroad,
That all might mark—knight, menial, high, and low—
An ordinance it concern'd them much to know.
If, after all, some headstrong hardy lout
Would disobey, though sure to be shut out,
Could he with reason murmur at his case,
Himself sole author of his own disgrace?
No! the decree was just and without flaw;
And he that made had right to make the law;
His sovereign power and pleasure unrestrain'd,
The wrong was his who wrongfully complain'd.
   Yet half mankind maintain a churlish strife
With him the Donor of eternal life,
Because the deed, by which his love confirms
The largess he bestows, prescribes the terms.
Compliance with his will your lot ensures,
Accept it only, and the boon is yours.
And sure it is as kind to smile and give,
As with a frown to say, Do this, and live.
Love is not pedlar's trumpery, bought and sold;
He will give freely, or he will withhold;
His soul abhors a mercenary thought,
And him as deeply who abhors it not;
He stipulates indeed, but merely this,
That man will freely take an unbought bliss,
Will trust him for a faithful generous part,
Nor set a price upon a willing heart.
Of all the ways that seem to promise fair,
To place you where his saints his presence share,
This only can; for this plain cause, express'd
In terms as plain—himself has shut the rest.
But oh the strife, the bickering, and debate,
The tidings of unpurchased heaven create!
The flirted fan, the bridle, and the toss,
All speakers, yet all language at a loss.
From stucco'd walls smart arguments rebound;
And beaus, adepts in every thing profound,
Die of disdain, or whistle off the sound.
Such is the clamour of rooks, daws, and kites,
The explosion of the levell'd tube excites,
Where mouldering abbey walls o'erhang the glade,
And oaks coeval spread a mournful shade,

The screaming nations, hovering in mid air,
Loudly resent the stranger's freedom there,
And seem to warn him never to repeat
His bold intrusion on their dark retreat.
  Adieu, Vinosa cries, ere yet he sips
The purple bumper trembling at his lips,
Adieu to all morality! if grace
Make works a vain ingredient in the case.
The Christian hope is—Waiter, draw the cork—
If I mistake not—Blockhead! with a fork!
Without good works, whatever some may boast,
Mere folly and delusion—Sir, your toast.
My firm persuasion is, at least sometimes,
That Heaven will weigh man's virtues and his crimes
With nice attention in a righteous scale,
And save or damn as these or those prevail.
I plant my foot upon this ground of trust,
And silence every fear with—God is just.
But if perchance, on some dull drizzling day,
A thought intrude, that says, or seems to say,
If thus the important cause is to be tried,
Suppose the beam should dip on the wrong side;
I soon recover from these needless frights,
And—God is merciful—sets all to rights.
Thus between justice, as my prime support,
And mercy, fled to as the last resort,
I glide and steal along with heaven in view,
And,—pardon me, the bottle stands with you.
  I never will believe, the Colonel cries,
The sanguinary schemes that some devise,
Who make the good Creator, on their plan,
A being of less equity than man.
If appetite, or what divines call lust,
Which men comply with, e'en because they must,
Be punish'd with perdition, who is pure?
Then theirs, no doubt, as well as mine, is sure.
If sentence of eternal pain belong
To every sudden slip and transient wrong,
Then Heaven enjoins the fallible and frail
A hopeless task, and damns them if they fail.
My creed, (whatever some creed-makers mean
By Athanasian nonsense, or Nicene,)
My creed is, he is safe that does his best,
And death's a doom sufficient for the rest.
  Right, says an ensign; and for aught I see,
Your faith and mine substantially agree;
The best of every man's performance here
Is to discharge the duties of his sphere.

A lawyer's dealings should be just and fair,
Honesty shines with great advantage there.
Fasting and prayer sit well upon a priest,
A decent caution and reserve at least.
A soldier's best is courage in the field,
With nothing here that wants to be conceal'd;
Manly deportment, gallant, easy, gay;
A hand as liberal as the light of day.
The soldier thus endow'd, who never shrinks,
Nor closets up his thoughts, whate'er he thinks,
Who scorns to do an injury by stealth,
Must go to heaven—and I must drink his health.
Sir Smug, he cries, (for lowest at the board,
Just made fifth chaplain of his patron lord,
His shoulders witnessing by many a shrug
How much his feelings suffered, sat Sir Smug,)
Your office is to winnow false from true;
Come, prophet, drink, and tell us, What think you?
   Sighing and smiling as he takes his glass,
Which they that woo preferment rarely pass,
Fallible man, the church-bred youth replies,
Is still found fallible, however wise;
And differing judgments serve but to declare,
That truth lies somewhere, if we knew but where.
Of all it ever was my lot to read,
Of critics now alive or long since dead,
The book of all the world that charm'd me most
Was,—well-a-day, the title-page was lost;
The writer well remarks, a heart that knows
To take with gratitude what Heaven bestows,
With prudence always ready at our call,
To guide our use of it, is all in all.
Doubtless it is. To which, of my own store,
I superadd a few essentials more;
But these, excuse the liberty I take,
I wave just now, for conversation's sake.
Spoke like an oracle, they all exclaim,
And add Right Reverend to Smug's honour'd name.
   And yet our lot is given us in a land
Where busy arts are never at a stand;
Where science points her telescopic eye,
Familiar with the wonders of the sky;
Where bold inquiry, diving out of sight,
Brings many a precious pearl of truth to light;
Where nought eludes the persevering quest,
That fashion, taste, or luxury suggest.
   But above all, in her own light array'd,
See Mercy's grand apocalypse display'd!

The sacred book no longer suffers wrong,
Bound in the fetters of an unknown tongue;
But speaks with plainness art could never mend,
What simplest minds can soonest comprehend.
God gives the word, the preachers throng around,
Live from his lips, and spread the glorious sound:
That sound bespeaks salvation on her way,
The trumpet of a life-restoring day;
'Tis heard where England's eastern glory shines,
And in the gulfs of her Cornubian mines.
And still it spreads. See Germany send forth
Her sons to pour it on the farthest north:
Fired with a zeal peculiar, they defy
The rage and rigour of a polar sky,
And plant successfully sweet Sharon's rose
On icy plains, and in eternal snows.
　　O blest within the inclosure of your rocks,
Not herds have ye to boast, nor bleating flocks;
Nor fertilizing streams your fields divide,
That show, reversed, the villas on their side;
No groves have ye; no cheerful sound of bird,
Or voice of turtle in your land is heard;
Nor grateful eglantine regales the smell
Of those that walk at evening where ye dwell;
But Winter, arm'd with terrors here unknown,
Sits absolute on his unshaken throne;
Piles up his stores amidst the frozen waste,
And bids the mountains he has built stand fast;
Beckons the legions of his storms away
From happier scenes, to make your land a prey;
Proclaims the soil a conquest he has won,
And scorns to share it with the distant sun.
—Yet truth is yours, remote, unenvied isle!
And peace the genuine offspring of her smile;
The pride of letter'd ignorance that binds
In chains of error our accomplish'd minds,
That decks, with all the splendour of the true,
A false religion, is unknown to you.
Nature indeed vouchsafes for our delight
The sweet vicissitudes of day and night;
Soft airs and genial moisture feed and cheer
Field, fruit, and flower, and every creature here;
But brighter beams than his who fires the skies
Have risen at length on your admiring eyes,
That shoot into your darkest caves the day,
From which our nicer optics turn away.
　　Here see the encouragement grace gives to vice,
The dire effect of mercy without price!

What were they? what some fools are made by art,
They were by nature, atheists, head and heart.
The gross idolatry blind heathens teach
Was too refined for them, beyond their reach.
Not e'en the glorious sun, though men revere
The monarch most that seldom will appear,
And though his beams, that quicken where they shine,
May claim some right to be esteem'd divine,
Not e'en the sun, desirable as rare,
Could bend one knee, engage one votary there;
They were, what base credulity believes
True Christians are, dissemblers, drunkards, thieves.
The full gorged savage, at his nauseous feast,
Spent half the darkness, and snored out the rest,
Was one, whom justice, on an equal plan,
Denouncing death upon the sins of man,
Might almost have indulged with an escape,
Chargeable only with a human shape.

   What are they now?—Morality may spare
Her grave concern, her kind suspicions there;
The wretch, who once sang wildly, danced, and laugh'd,
And suck'd in dizzy madness with his draught,
Has wept a silent flood, reversed his ways,
Is sober, meek, benevolent, and prays,
Feeds sparingly, communicates his store,
Abhors the craft he boasted of before,
And he that stole has learn'd to steal no more.
Well spake the prophet, Let the desert sing,
Where sprang the thorn, the spiry fir shall spring,
And where unsightly and rank thistles grew,
Shall grow the myrtle and luxuriant yew.

   Go now, and with important tone demand
On what foundation virtue is to stand,
If self-exalting claims be turn'd adrift,
And grace be grace indeed, and life a gift;
The poor reclaim'd inhabitant, his eyes
Glistening at once with pity and surprise,
Amazed that shadows should obscure the sight
Of one, whose birth was in a land of light,
Shall answer, Hope, sweet Hope, has set me free,
And made all pleasures else mere dross to me.

   These, amidst scenes as waste as if denied
The common care that waits on all beside,
Wild as if nature there, void of all good,
Play'd only gambols in a frantic mood,
(Yet charge not heavenly skill with having plann'd
A plaything world, unworthy of his hand;)
Can see his love, though secret evil lurks

In all we touch, stamp'd plainly on his works;
Deem life a blessing with its numerous woes,
Nor spurn away a gift a God bestows.
Hard task indeed o'er arctic seas to roam!
Is hope exotic? grows it not at home?
Yes, but an object, bright as orient morn,
May press the eye too closely to be borne;
A distant virtue we can all confess,
It hurts our pride, and moves our envy, less.
  Leuconomus (beneath well-sounding Greek
I slur a name a poet must not speak)
Stood pilloried on infamy's high stage,
And bore the pelting scorn of half an age;
The very butt of slander, and the blot
For every dart that malice ever shot.
The man that mention'd him at once dismiss'd
All mercy from his lips, and sneer'd and hiss'd;
His crimes were such as Sodom never knew,
And perjury stood up to swear all true;
His aim was mischief, and his zeal pretence,
His speech rebellion against common sense;
A knave, when tried on honesty's plain rule;
And when by that of reason, a mere fool;
The world's best comfort was, his doom was pass'd;
Die when he might, he must be damn'd at last.
  Now, Truth, perform thine office; waft aside
The curtain drawn by prejudice and pride,
Reveal (the man is dead) to wondering eyes
This more than monster in his proper guise.
He loved the world that hated him: the tear
That dropp'd upon his Bible was sincere;
Assail'd by scandal and the tongue of strife,
His only answer was a blameless life;
And he that forged, and he that threw the dart,
Had each a brother's interest in his heart.
Paul's love of Christ, and steadiness unbribed,
Were copied close in him, and well transcribed.
He followed Paul; his zeal a kindred flame,
His apostolic charity the same.
Like him, cross'd cheerfully tempestuous seas,
Forsaking country, kindred, friends, and ease;
Like him he labour'd, and like him content
To bear it, suffered shame where'er he went.
Blush, calumny! and write upon his tomb,
If honest eulogy can spare thee room,
Thy deep repentance of thy thousand lies,
Which, aim'd at him, have pierced the offended skies;
And say, Blot out my sin, confess'd, deplored,

Against thine image, in thy saint, O Lord!
   No blinder bigot, I maintain it still,
Than he who must have pleasure, come what will:
He laughs, whatever weapon Truth may draw,
And deems her sharp artillery mere straw;
Scripture indeed is plain; but God and he
On scripture ground are sure to disagree;
Some wiser rule must teach him how to live,
Than this his Maker has seen fit to give;
Supple and flexible as Indian cane,
To take the bend his appetites ordain;
Contrived to suit frail nature's crazy case,
And reconcile his lusts with saving grace.
By this, with nice precision of design,
He draws upon life's map a zig-zag line,
That shows how far 'tis safe to follow sin,
And where his danger and God's wrath begin.
By this he forms, as pleased he sports along,
His well-poised estimate of right and wrong;
And finds the modish manners of the day,
Though loose, as harmless as an infant's play.
   Build by whatever plan caprice decrees,
With what materials, on what ground you please;
Your hope shall stand unblamed, perhaps admired,
If not that hope the scripture has required.
The strange conceits, vain projects, and wild dreams,
With which hypocrisy for ever teems,
(Though other follies strike the public eye,
And raise a laugh) pass unmolested by;
But if, unblameable in word and thought,
A MAN arise, a man whom God has taught,
With all Elijah's dignity of tone,
And all the love of the beloved John,
To storm the citadels they build in air,
And smite the untemper'd wall; 'tis death to spare.
To sweep away all refuges of lies,
And place, instead of quirks themselves devise,
Lama sabacthani before their eyes;
To prove that without Christ all gain is loss,
All hope despair, that stands not on his cross;
Except the few his God may have impress'd,
A tenfold frenzy seizes all the rest.
   Throughout mankind, the Christian kind at least,
There dwells a consciousness in every breast,
That folly ends where genuine hope begins,
And he that finds his heaven must lose his sins.
Nature opposes, with her utmost force,
This riving stroke, this ultimate divorce:

And, while Religion seems to be her view,
Hates with a deep sincerity the true:
For this, of all that ever influenced man,
Since Abel worshipp'd, or the world began,
This only spares no lust, admits no plea,
But makes him, if at all, completely free;
Sounds forth the signal, as she mounts her car,
Of an eternal, universal war;
Rejects all treaty, penetrates all wiles,
Scorns with the same indifference frowns and smiles;
Drives through the realms of sin, where riot reels,
And grinds his crown beneath her burning wheels!
Hence all that is in man, pride, passion, art,
Powers of the mind, and feelings of the heart,
Insensible of truth's almighty charms,
Starts at her first approach, and sounds to arms!
While Bigotry, with well dissembled fears,
His eyes shut fast, his fingers in his ears,
Mighty to parry and push by God's word
With senseless noise, his argument the sword,
Pretends a zeal for godliness and grace,
And spits abhorrence in the Christian's face.
   Parent of Hope, immortal Truth! make known
Thy deathless wreaths and triumphs all thine own:
The silent progress of thy power is such,
Thy means so feeble, and despised so much,
That few believe the wonders thou hast wrought,
And none can teach them but whom thou hast taught.
Oh see me sworn to serve thee, and command
A painter's skill into a poet's hand!
That, while I trembling trace a work divine,
Fancy may stand aloof from the design,
And light and shade, and every stroke, be thine.
   If ever thou hast felt another's pain,
If ever when he sighed hast sighed again,
If ever on thy eyelid stood the tear
That pity had engender'd, drop one here.
This man was happy—had the world's good word,
And with it every joy it can afford;
Friendship and love seem'd tenderly at strife,
Which most should sweeten his untroubled life;
Politely learn'd, and of a gentle race,
Good breeding and good sense gave all a grace,
And whether at the toilette of the fair
He laugh'd and trifled, made him welcome there,
Or, if in masculine debate he shared,
Ensured him mute attention and regard.
Alas, how changed! Expressive of his mind,

His eyes are sunk, arms folded, head reclined;
Those awful syllables, hell, death, and sin,
Though whisper'd, plainly tell what works within;
That conscience there performs her proper part,
And writes a doomsday sentence on his heart!
Forsaking and forsaken of all friends,
He now perceives where earthly pleasure ends;
Hard task! for one who lately knew no care,
And harder still as learnt beneath despair!
His hours no longer pass unmark'd away,
A dark importance saddens every day;
He hears the notice of the clock, perplex'd,
And cries, Perhaps eternity strikes next!
Sweet music is no longer music here,
And laughter sounds like madness in his ear:
His grief the world of all her power disarms;
Wine has no taste, and beauty has no charms:
God's holy word, once trivial in his view,
Now by the voice of his experience true,
Seems, as it is, the fountain whence alone
Must spring that hope he pants to make his own.
   Now let the bright reverse be known abroad;
Say man's a worm, and power belongs to God.
As when a felon, whom his country's laws
Have justly doom'd for some atrocious cause,
Expects, in darkness and heart-chilling fears,
The shameful close of all his misspent years;
If chance, on heavy pinions slowly borne,
A tempest usher in the dreaded morn,
Upon his dungeon walls the lightning play,
The thunder seems to summon him away;
The warder at the door his key applies,
Shoots back the bolt, and all his courage dies:
If then, just then, all thoughts of mercy lost,
When Hope, long lingering, at last yields the ghost,
The sound of pardon pierce his startled ear,
He drops at once his fetters and his fear;
A transport glows in all he looks and speaks,
And the first thankful tears bedew his cheeks.
Joy, far superior joy, that much outweighs
The comfort of a few poor added days,
Invades, possesses, and o'erwhelms the soul
Of him, whom Hope has with a touch made whole.
'Tis heaven, all heaven, descending on the wings
Of the glad legions of the King of kings;
'Tis more—'tis God diffused through every part,
'Tis God himself triumphant in his heart.
O welcome now the sun's once hated light,

His noonday beams were never half so bright.
Not kindred minds alone are call'd to employ
Their hours, their days, in listening to his joy;
Unconscious nature, all that he surveys,
Rocks, groves, and streams must join him in his praise.
   These are thy glorious works, eternal Truth,
The scoff of wither'd age and beardless youth;
These move the censure and illiberal grin
Of fools that hate thee and delight in sin:
But these shall last when night has quench'd the pole,
And heav'n is all departed as a scroll.
And when, as justice has long since decreed,
This earth shall blaze, and a new world succeed,
Then these thy glorious works, and they who share
That hope which can alone exclude despair,
Shall live exempt from weakness and decay,
The brightest wonders of an endless day.
   Happy the bard (if that fair name belong
To him that blends no fable with his song)
Whose lines, uniting, by an honest art,
The faithful monitor's and poet's part,
Seek to delight, that they may mend mankind,
And, while they captivate inform the mind:
Still happier, if he till a thankful soil,
And fruit reward his honourable toil:
But happier far, who comfort those that wait
To hear plain truth at Judah's hallow'd gate:
Their language simple, as their manners meek,
No shining ornaments have they to seek;
Nor labour they, nor time, nor talents, waste,
In sorting flowers to suit a fickle taste;
But, while they speak the wisdom of the skies,
Which art can only darken and disguise,
The abundant harvest, recompense divine,
Repays their work—the gleaning only mine.

CHARITY

Qua nihil majus meliusve terris
Fata donavêre, bonique divi;
Nec dabunt, quamvis redeant in aurum
Tempora priscum.
Hor. lib. iv. Ode 2.

THE ARGUMENT

Fairest and foremost of the train that wait
On man's most dignified and happiest state,
Whether we name thee Charity or Love,
Chief grace below, and all in all above,
Prosper (I press thee with a powerful plea)
A task I venture on, impell'd by thee:
Oh never seen but in thy blest effects,
Or felt but in the soul that Heaven selects;
Who seeks to praise thee, and to make thee known
To other hearts, must have thee in his own.
Come, prompt me with benevolent desires,
Teach me to kindle at thy gentle fires,
And, though disgraced and slighted, to redeem
A poet's name, by making thee the theme.
   God, working ever on a social plan,
By various ties attaches man to man:
He made at first, though free and unconfined,
One man the common father of the kind;
That every tribe, though placed as he sees best,
Where seas or deserts part them from the rest,
Differing in language, manners, or in face,
Might feel themselves allied to all the race.
When Cook—lamented, and with tears as just
As ever mingled with heroic dust—
Steer'd Britain's oak into a world unknown,
And in his country's glory sought his own,
Wherever he found man to nature true,
The rights of man were sacred in his view;
He soothed with gifts, and greeted with a smile,
The simple native of the new-found isle;
He spurn'd the wretch that slighted or withstood
The tender argument of kindred blood;
Nor would endure that any should control
His freeborn brethren of the southern pole.
   But, though some nobler minds a law respect,
That none shall with impunity neglect,
In baser souls unnumber'd evils meet,
To thwart its influence, and its end defeat.

While Cook is loved for savage lives he saved,
See Cortez odious for a world enslaved!
Where wast thou then, sweet Charity? where then,
Thou tutelary friend of helpless men?
Wast thou in monkish cells and nunneries found,
Or building hospitals on English ground?
No.—Mammon makes the world his legatee
Through fear, not love; and Heaven abhors the fee.
Wherever found, (and all men need thy care,)
Nor age nor infancy could find thee there.
The hand that slew till it could slay no more
Was glued to the sword-hilt with Indian gore.
Their prince, as justly seated on his throne
As vain imperial Philip on his own,
Trick'd out of all his royalty by art,
That stripp'd him bare, and broke his honest heart,
Died, by the sentence of a shaven priest,
For scorning what they taught him to detest.
How dark the veil that intercepts the blaze
Of Heaven's mysterious purposes and ways!
God stood not, though he seem'd to stand, aloof;
And at this hour the conqueror feels the proof:
The wreath he won drew down an instant curse,
The fretting plague is in the public purse,
The canker'd spoil corrodes the pining state,
Starved by that indolence their mines create.
   Oh could their ancient Incas rise again,
How would they take up Israel's taunting strain!
Art thou too fallen, Iberia? Do we see
The robber and the murderer weak as we?
Thou, that hast wasted earth, and dared despise
Alike the wrath and mercy of the skies,
Thy pomp is in the grave, thy glory laid
Low in the pits thine avarice has made.
We come with joy from our eternal rest
To see the oppressor in his turn oppress'd.
Art thou the god, the thunder of whose hand
Roll'd over all our desolated land,
Shook principalities and kingdoms down,
And made the mountains tremble at his frown?
The sword shall light upon thy boasted powers,
And waste them, as thy sword has wasted ours.
'Tis thus Omnipotence his law fulfils,
And vengeance executes what justice wills.
   Again—the band of commerce was designed
To associate all the branches of mankind;
And if a boundless plenty be the robe,
Trade is the golden girdle of the globe.

Wise to promote whatever end he means,
God opens fruitful Nature's various scenes:
Each climate needs what other climes produce,
And offers something to the general use;
No land but listens to the common call,
And in return receives supply from all.
This genial intercourse, and mutual aid,
Cheers what were else a universal shade,
Calls nature from her ivy-mantled den,
And softens human rock-work into men.
Ingenious Art, with her expressive face,
Steps forth to fashion and refine the race;
Not only fills necessity's demand,
But overcharges her capacious hand:
Capricious taste itself can crave no more
Than she supplies from her abounding store:
She strikes out all that luxury can ask,
And gains new vigour at her endless task.
Hers is the spacious arch, the shapely spire,
The painter's pencil, and the poet's lyre;
From her the canvas borrows light and shade,
And verse, more lasting, hues that never fade.
She guides the finger o'er the dancing keys,
Gives difficulty all the grace of ease,
And pours a torrent of sweet notes around
Fast as the thirsting ear can drink the sound.
    These are the gifts of art; and art thrives most
Where Commerce has enrich'd the busy coast;
He catches all improvements in his flight,
Spreads foreign wonders in his country's sight,
Imports what others have invented well,
And stirs his own to match them, or excel.
'Tis thus, reciprocating each with each,
Alternately the nations learn and teach;
While Providence enjoins to every soul
A union with the vast terraqueous whole.
    Heaven speed the canvas, gallantly unfurl'd
To furnish and accommodate a world,
To give the pole the produce of the sun,
And knit the unsocial climates into one.
Soft airs and gentle heavings of the wave
Impel the fleet, whose errand is to save,
To succour wasted regions, and replace
The smile of opulence in sorrow's face.
Let nothing adverse, nothing unforeseen,
Impede the bark that ploughs the deep serene,
Charged with a freight transcending in its worth
The gems of India, Nature's rarest birth,

That flies, like Gabriel on his Lord's commands,
A herald of God's love to pagan lands!
But ah! what wish can prosper, or what prayer,
For merchants rich in cargoes of despair,
Who drive a loathsome traffic, gauge, and span,
And buy the muscles and the bones of man?
The tender ties of father, husband, friend,
All bonds of nature in that moment end;
And each endures, while yet he draws his breath,
A stroke as fatal as the scythe of death.
The sable warrior, frantic with regret
Of her he loves, and never can forget,
Loses in tears the far receding shore,
But not the thought that they must meet no more;
Deprived of her and freedom at a blow,
What has he left that he can yet forego?
Yes, to deep sadness sullenly resign'd,
He feels his body's bondage in his mind;
Puts off his generous nature, and, to suit
His manners with his fate, puts on the brute.
  Oh most degrading of all ills that wait
On man, a mourner in his best estate!
All other sorrows virtue may endure,
And find submission more than half a cure;
Grief is itself a medicine, and bestow'd
To improve the fortitude that bears the load;
To teach the wanderer, as his woes increase,
The path of wisdom, all whose paths are peace;
But slavery!—Virtue dreads it as her grave:
Patience itself is meanness in a slave;
Or, if the will and sovereignty of God
Bid suffer it awhile, and kiss the rod,
Wait for the dawning of a brighter day,
And snap the chain the moment when you may.
Nature imprints upon whate'er we see,
That has a heart and life in it, Be free!
The beasts are charter'd—neither age nor force
Can quell the love of freedom in a horse:
He breaks the cord that held him at the rack;
And, conscious of an unincumber'd back,
Snuffs up the morning air, forgets the rein;
Loose fly his forelock and his ample mane;
Responsive to the distant neigh he neighs;
Nor stops, till, overleaping all delays,
He finds the pasture where his fellows graze.
  Canst thou, and honour'd with a Christian name,
Buy what is woman-born, and feel no shame?
Trade in the blood of innocence, and plead

Expedience as a warrant for the deed?
So may the wolf, whom famine has made bold
To quit the forest and invade the fold:
So may the ruffian, who with ghostly glide,
Dagger in hand, steals close to your bedside;
Not he, but his emergence forced the door,
He found it inconvenient to be poor.
Has God then given its sweetness to the cane,
Unless his laws be trampled on—in vain?
Built a brave world, which cannot yet subsist,
Unless his right to rule it be dismiss'd?
Impudent blasphemy! So folly pleads,
And, avarice being judge, with ease succeeds.
   But grant the plea, and let it stand for just,
That man make man his prey, because he must;
Still there is room for pity to abate
And soothe the sorrows of so sad a state.
A Briton knows, or if he knows it not,
The scripture placed within his reach, he ought,
That souls have no discriminating hue,
Alike important in their Maker's view;
That none are free from blemish since the fall,
And love divine has paid one price for all.
The wretch that works and weeps without relief
Has One that notices his silent grief.
He, from whose hand alone all power proceeds,
Ranks its abuse among the foulest deeds,
Considers all injustice with a frown;
But marks the man that treads his fellow down.
Begone!—the whip and bell in that hard hand
Are hateful ensigns of usurp'd command.
Not Mexico could purchase kings a claim
To scourge him, weariness his only blame.
Remember, Heaven has an avenging rod,
To smite the poor is treason against God!
   Trouble is grudgingly and hardly brook'd,
While life's sublimest joys are overlook'd:
We wander o'er a sun-burnt thirsty soil,
Murmuring and weary of our daily toil,
Forget to enjoy the palm-tree's offer'd shade,
Or taste the fountain in the neighbouring glade:
Else who would lose, that had the power to improve
The occasion of transmuting fear to love?
Oh 'tis a godlike privilege to save!
And he that scorns it is himself a slave.
Inform his mind; one flash of heavenly day
Would heal his heart, and melt his chains away.
"Beauty for ashes" is a gift indeed,

And slaves, by truth enlarged, are doubly freed.
Then would he say, submissive at thy feet,
While gratitude and love made service sweet,
My dear deliverer out of hopeless night,
Whose bounty bought me but to give me light,
I was a bondman on my native plain,
Sin forged, and ignorance made fast, the chain;
Thy lips have shed instruction as the dew,
Taught me what path to shun, and what pursue;
Farewell my former joys! I sigh no more
For Africa's once loved, benighted shore;
Serving a benefactor, I am free;
At my best home, if not exiled from thee.
   Some men make gain a fountain whence proceeds
A stream of liberal and heroic deeds;
The swell of pity, not to be confined
Within the scanty limits of the mind,
Disdains the bank, and throws the golden sands,
A rich deposit, on the bordering lands:
These have an ear for his paternal call,
Who makes some rich for the supply of all;
God's gift with pleasure in his praise employ;
And Thornton is familiar with the joy.
   Oh could I worship aught beneath the skies
That earth has seen, or fancy can devise,
Thine altar, sacred Liberty, should stand,
Built by no mercenary vulgar hand,
With fragrant turf, and flowers as wild and fair
As ever dress'd a bank, or scented summer air.
Duly, as ever on the mountain's height
The peep of morning shed a dawning light,
Again, when evening in her sober vest
Drew the grey curtain of the fading west,
My soul should yield thee willing thanks and praise
For the chief blessings of my fairest days:
But that were sacrilege—praise is not thine,
But his who gave thee, and preserves thee mine:
Else I would say, and as I spake bid fly
A captive bird into the boundless sky,
This triple realm adores thee—thou art come
From Sparta hither, and art here at home.
We feel thy force still active, at this hour
Enjoy immunity from priestly power,
While conscience, happier than in ancient years,
Owns no superior but the God she fears.
Propitious spirit! yet expunge a wrong
Thy rights have suffer'd, and our land, too long.
Teach mercy to ten thousand hearts, that share

The fears and hopes of a commercial care.
Prisons expect the wicked, and were built
To bind the lawless, and to punish guilt;
But shipwreck, earthquake, battle, fire, and flood,
Are mighty mischiefs, not to be withstood;
And honest merit stands on slippery ground,
Where covert guile and artifice abound.
Let just restraint, for public peace design'd,
Chain up the wolves and tigers of mankind;
The foe of virtue has no claim to thee,
But let insolvent innocence go free.

   Patron of else the most despised of men,
Accept the tribute of a stranger's pen;
Verse, like the laurel, its immortal meed,
Should be the guerdon of a noble deed;
I may alarm thee, but I fear the shame
(Charity chosen as my theme and aim)
I must incur, forgetting Howard's name.
Blest with all wealth can give thee, to resign
Joys doubly sweet to feelings quick as thine,
To quit the bliss thy rural scenes bestow,
To seek a nobler amidst scenes of woe,
To traverse seas, range kingdoms, and bring home,
Not the proud monuments of Greece or Rome,
But knowledge such as only dungeons teach,
And only sympathy like thine could reach;
That grief, sequester'd from the public stage,
Might smooth her feathers, and enjoy her cage;
Speaks a divine ambition, and a zeal,
The boldest patriot might be proud to feel.
Oh that the voice of clamour and debate,
That pleads for peace till it disturbs the state,
Were hush'd in favour of thy generous plea,
The poor thy clients, and Heaven's smile thy fee!

   Philosophy, that does not dream or stray,
Walks arm in arm with nature all his way;
Compasses earth, dives into it, ascends
Whatever steep inquiry recommends,
Sees planetary wonders smoothly roll
Round other systems under her control,
Drinks wisdom at the milky stream of light,
That cheers the silent journey of the night,
And brings at his return a bosom charged
With rich instruction, and a soul enlarged.
The treasured sweets of the capacious plan,
That Heaven spreads wide before the view of man.
All prompt his pleased pursuit, and to pursue
Still prompt him, with a pleasure always new;

He too has a connecting power, and draws
Man to the centre of the common cause,
Aiding a dubious and deficient sight
With a new medium and a purer light.
All truth is precious, if not all divine;
And what dilates the powers must needs refine.
He reads the skies, and, watching every change,
Provides the faculties an ampler range;
And wins mankind, as his attempts prevail,
A prouder station on the general scale.
But reason still, unless divinely taught,
Whate'er she learns, learns nothing as she ought;
The lamp of revelation only shows,
What human wisdom cannot but oppose,
That man, in nature's richest mantle clad,
And graced with all philosophy can add,
Though fair without, and luminous within
Is still the progeny and heir of sin.
Thus taught, down falls the plumage of his pride;
He feels his need of an unerring guide,
And knows that falling he shall rise no more,
Unless the power that bade him stand restore.
This is indeed philosophy; this known
Makes wisdom, worthy of the name, his own;
And without this, whatever he discuss;
Whether the space between the stars and us;
Whether he measure earth, compute the sea,
Weigh sunbeams, carve a fly, or spit a flea;
The solemn trifler with his boasted skill
Toils much, and is a solemn trifler still:
Blind was he born, and his misguided eyes
Grown dim in trifling studies, blind he dies.
Self-knowledge truly learn'd of course implies
The rich possession of a nobler prize;
For self to self, and God to man, reveal'd,
(Two themes to nature's eye for ever seal'd,)
Are taught by rays, that fly with equal pace
From the same centre of enlightening grace.
Here stay thy foot; how copious, and how clear,
The o'erflowing well of Charity springs here!
Hark! 'tis the music of a thousand rills,
Some through the groves, some down the sloping hills,
Winding a secret or an open course,
And all supplied from an eternal source.
The ties of nature do but feebly bind,
And commerce partially reclaims mankind;
Philosophy, without his heavenly guide,
May blow up self-conceit, and nourish pride;

But, while his province is the reasoning part,
Has still a veil of midnight on his heart:
'Tis truth divine, exhibited on earth,
Gives Charity her being and her birth.
   Suppose (when thought is warm, and fancy flows,
What will not argument sometimes suppose?)
An isle possessed by creatures of our kind,
Endued with reason, yet by nature blind.
Let supposition lend her aid once more,
And land some grave optician on the shore:
He claps his lens, if haply they may see,
Close to the part where vision ought to be;
But finds that, though his tubes assist the sight,
They cannot give it, or make darkness light.
He reads wise lectures, and describes aloud
A sense they know not to the wondering crowd;
He talks of light and the prismatic hues,
As men of depth in erudition use;
But all he gains for his harangue is—Well,——
What monstrous lies some travellers will tell!
   The soul, whose sight all-quickening grace renews,
Takes the resemblance of the good she views,
As diamonds, stripp'd of their opaque disguise,
Reflect the noon-day glory of the skies.
She speaks of Him, her author, guardian, friend,
Whose love knew no beginning, knows no end,
In language warm as all that love inspires;
And, in the glow of her intense desires,
Pants to communicate her noble fires.
She sees a world stark blind to what employs
Her eager thought, and feeds her flowing joys;
Though wisdom hail them, heedless of her call,
Flies to save some, and feels a pang for all:
Herself as weak as her support is strong,
She feels that frailty she denied so long;
And, from a knowledge of her own disease,
Learns to compassionate the sick she sees.
Here see, acquitted of all vain pretence,
The reign of genuine Charity commence.
Though scorn repay her sympathetic tears,
She still is kind, and still she perseveres;
The truth she loves a sightless world blaspheme,
'Tis childish dotage, a delirious dream!
The danger they discern not they deny;
Laugh at their only remedy, and die.
But still a soul thus touch'd can never cease,
Whoever threatens war, to speak of peace.
Pure in her aim, and in her temper mild,

Her wisdom seems the weakness of a child:
She makes excuses where she might condemn,
Reviled by those that hate her, prays for them;
Suspicion lurks not in her artless breast,
The worst suggested, she believes the best;
Not soon provoked, however stung and teased,
And, if perhaps made angry, soon appeased;
She rather waives than will dispute her right;
And, injured, makes forgiveness her delight.
   Such was the portrait an apostle drew,
The bright original was one he knew;
Heaven held his hand, the likeness must be true.
   When one, that holds communion with the skies,
Has fill'd his urn where these pure waters rise,
And once more mingles with us meaner things,
'Tis e'en as if an angel shook his wings;
Immortal fragrance fills the circuit wide,
That tells us whence his treasures are supplied.
So when a ship, well freighted with the stores
The sun matures on India's spicy shores,
Has dropp'd her anchor, and her canvas furl'd,
In some safe haven of our western world,
'Twere vain inquiry to what port she went,
The gale informs us, laden with the scent.
   Some seek, when queasy conscience has its qualms,
To lull the painful malady with alms;
But charity not feign'd intends alone
Another's good—theirs centres in their own;
And, too short-lived to reach the realms of peace,
Must cease for ever when the poor shall cease.
Flavia, most tender of her own good name,
Is rather careless of her sister's fame:
Her superfluity the poor supplies,
But, if she touch a character, it dies.
The seeming virtue weigh'd against the vice,
She deems all safe, for she has paid the price:
No charity but alms aught values she,
Except in porcelain on her mantel-tree.
How many deeds, with which the world has rung,
From pride, in league with ignorance, have sprung!
But God o'errules all human follies still,
And bends the tough materials to his will.
A conflagration, or a wintry flood,
Has left some hundreds without home or food:
Extravagance and avarice shall subscribe,
While fame and self-complacence are the bribe.
The brief proclaim'd, it visits every pew,
But first the squire's, a compliment but due:

With slow deliberation he unties
His glittering purse, that envy of all eyes!
And, while the clerk just puzzles out the psalm,
Slides guinea behind guinea in his palm;
Till finding, what he might have found before,
A smaller piece amidst the precious store,
Pinch'd close between his finger and his thumb,
He half exhibits, and then drops the sum.
Gold, to be sure!—Throughout the town 'tis told
How the good squire gives never less than gold.
From motives such as his, though not the best,
Springs in due time supply for the distress'd;
Not less effectual than what love bestows,
Except that office clips it as it goes.

   But lest I seem to sin against a friend,
And wound the grace I mean to recommend,
(Though vice derided with a just design
Implies no trespass against love divine,)
Once more I would adopt the graver style,
A teacher should be sparing of his smile.
Unless a love of virtue light the flame,
Satire is, more than those he brands, to blame:
He hides behind a magisterial air
His own offences, and strips others bare;
Affects indeed a most humane concern,
That men, if gently tutor'd, will not learn;
That mulish folly, not to be reclaim'd
By softer methods, must be made ashamed;
But (I might instance in St. Patrick's dean)
Too often rails to gratify his spleen.
Most satirists are indeed a public scourge;
Their mildest physic is a farrier's purge;
Their acrid temper turns, as soon as stirr'd,
The milk of their good purpose all to curd.
Their zeal begotten, as their works rehearse,
By lean despair upon an empty purse,
The wild assassins start into the street,
Prepared to poniard whomsoe'er they meet.
No skill in swordsmanship, however just,
Can be secure against a madman's thrust;
And even virtue, so unfairly match'd,
Although immortal, may be prick'd or scratch'd.
When scandal has new minted an old lie,
Or tax'd invention for a fresh supply,
'Tis call'd a satire, and the world appears
Gathering around it with erected ears:
A thousand names are toss'd into the crowd;
Some whisper'd softly, and some twang'd aloud,

Just as the sapience of an author's brain
Suggests it safe or dangerous to be plain.
Strange! how the frequent interjected dash
Quickens a market, and helps off the trash;
The important letters that include the rest,
Serve as a key to those that are suppress'd;
Conjecture gripes the victims in his paw,
The world is charm'd, and Scrib escapes the law.
So, when the cold damp shades of night prevail,
Worms may be caught by either head or tail;
Forcibly drawn from many a close recess,
They meet with little pity, no redress;
Plung'd in the stream, they lodge upon the mud,
Food for the famish'd rovers of the flood.
    All zeal for a reform, that gives offence
To peace and charity, is mere pretence:
A bold remark; but which, if well applied,
Would humble many a towering poet's pride.
Perhaps the man was in a sportive fit,
And had no other play-place for his wit;
Perhaps, enchanted with the love of fame,
He sought the jewel in his neighbour's shame;
Perhaps—whatever end he might pursue,
The cause of virtue could not be his view.
At every stroke wit flashes in our eyes;
The turns are quick, the polish'd points surprise,
But shine with cruel and tremendous charms,
That, while they please, possess us with alarms;
So have I seen, (and hasten'd to the sight
On all the wings of holiday delight,)
Where stands that monument of ancient power,
Named with emphatic dignity, the Tower,
Guns, halberts, swords, and pistols, great and small,
In starry forms disposed upon the wall:
We wonder, as we gazing stand below,
That brass and steel should make so fine a show;
But, though we praise the exact designer's skill,
Account them implements of mischief still.
    No works shall find acceptance in that day,
When all disguises shall be rent away,
That square not truly with the scripture plan,
Nor spring from love to God, or love to man.
As he ordains things sordid in their birth
To be resolved into their parent earth;
And, though the soul shall seek superior orbs,
Whate'er this world produces, it absorbs;
So self starts nothing, but what tends apace
Home to the goal, where it began the race.

Such as our motive is our aim must be;
If this be servile, that can ne'er be free:
If self employ us, whatsoe'er is wrought,
We glorify that self, not Him we ought;
Such virtues had need prove their own reward,
The Judge of all men owes them no regard.
True Charity, a plant divinely nursed,
Fed by the love from which it rose at first,
Thrives against hope, and, in the rudest scene,
Storms but enliven its unfading green;
Exuberant is the shadow it supplies,
Its fruit on earth, its growth above the skies.
To look at Him, who form'd us and redeem'd,
So glorious now, though once so disesteem'd;
To see a God stretch forth his human hand,
To uphold the boundless scenes of his command;
To recollect that, in a form like ours,
He bruised beneath his feet the infernal powers,
Captivity led captive, rose to claim
The wreath he won so dearly in our name;
That, throned above all height, he condescends
To call the few that trust in him his friends;
That, in the heaven of heavens, that space he deems
Too scanty for the exertion of his beams,
And shines, as if impatient to bestow
Life and a kingdom upon worms below;
That sight imparts a never-dying flame,
Though feeble in degree, in kind the same.
Like him the soul, thus kindled from above,
Spreads wide her arms of universal love;
And, still enlarged as she receives the grace,
Includes creation in her close embrace.
Behold a Christian!—and without the fires
The Founder of that name alone inspires,
Though all accomplishment, all knowledge meet,
To make the shining prodigy complete,
Whoever boasts that name—behold a cheat!
Were love, in these the world's last doting years,
As frequent as the want of it appears,
The churches warm'd, they would no longer hold
Such frozen figures, stiff as they are cold;
Relenting forms would lose their power, or cease;
And e'en the dipp'd and sprinkled live in peace:
Each heart would quit its prison in the breast,
And flow in free communion with the rest.
The statesman, skill'd in projects dark and deep,
Might burn his useless Machiavel, and sleep:
His budget, often fill'd, yet always poor,

Might swing at ease behind his study door,
No longer prey upon our annual rents,
Or scare the nation with its big contents:
Disbanded legions freely might depart,
And slaying man would cease to be an art.
No learned disputants would take the field,
Sure not to conquer, and sure not to yield;
Both sides deceived, if rightly understood,
Pelting each other for the public good.
Did Charity prevail, the press would prove
A vehicle of virtue, truth, and love;
And I might spare myself the pains to show
What few can learn, and all suppose they know.
   Thus have I sought to grace a serious lay
With many a wild, indeed, but flowery spray,
In hopes to gain, what else I must have lost,
The attention pleasure has so much engross'd.
But if unhappily deceived I dream,
And prove too weak for so divine a theme,
Let Charity forgive me a mistake,
That zeal, not vanity, has chanced to make,
And spare the poet for his subject's sake.

CONVERSATION

Nam neque me tantum venientis sibilus austri,
Nec percussa juvant fluctu tam litora, nec quæ
Saxosas inter decurrunt flumina valles.
Virg. Ecl. 5.

THE ARGUMENT

In conversation much depends on culture—Its results frequently insignificant—Indecent language and oaths reprobated—The author's dislike of the clash of arguments—The noisy wrangler—Dubius an example of indecision—The positive pronounce without hesitation—The point of honour condemned—Duelling with fists instead of weapons proposed—Effect of long tales—The retailer of prodigies and lies—Qualities of a judicious tale—Smoking condemned—The emphatic speaker—The perfumed beau—The grave coxcomb—Sickness made a topic of conversation—Picture of a fretful temper—The bashful speaker—An English company—The sportsman—Influence of fashion on conversation—Converse of the two disciples going to Emmaus—Delights of religious conversation—Age mellows the speech—True piety often branded as fanatic frenzy—Pleasure of communion with the good—Conversation should be unconstrained—Persons who make the Bible their companion, charged with hypocrisy by the world—The charge repelled—The poet sarcastically surmises that his censure of the world may proceed from ignorance of its reformed manners—An apology for digression—Religion purifies and enriches conversation.

Though nature weigh our talents, and dispense
To every man his modicum of sense,
And Conversation in its better part
May be esteem'd a gift, and not an art,
Yet much depends, as in the tiller's toil,
On culture, and the sowing of the soil.
Words learn'd by rote a parrot may rehearse,
But talking is not always to converse;
Not more distinct from harmony divine,
The constant creaking of a country sign.
As alphabets in ivory employ,
Hour after hour, the yet unletter'd boy,
Sorting and puzzling with a deal of glee
Those seeds of science call'd his A B C;
So language in the mouths of the adult,
Witness its insignificant result,
Too often proves an implement of play,
A toy to sport with, and pass time away.
Collect at evening what the day brought forth,
Compress the sum into its solid worth,
And if it weigh the importance of a fly,
The scales are false, or algebra a lie.
Sacred interpreter of human thought,
How few respect or use thee as they ought!
But all shall give account of every wrong,
Who dare dishonour or defile the tongue;
Who prostitute it in the cause of vice,
Or sell their glory at a market-price;
Who vote for hire, or point it with lampoon,
The dear-bought placeman, and the cheap buffoon.
   There is a prurience in the speech of some,
Wrath stays him, or else God would strike them dumb:
His wise forbearance has their end in view,
They fill their measure, and receive their due.
The heathen lawgivers of ancient days,
Names almost worthy of a Christian's praise,
Would drive them forth from the resort of men,
And shut up every satyr in his den.
Oh come not ye near innocence and truth,
Ye worms that eat into the bud of youth!
Infectious as impure, your blighting power
Taints in its rudiments the promised flower;
Its odour perish'd and its charming hue,
Thenceforth 'tis hateful, for it smells of you.
Not e'en the vigorous and headlong rage
Of adolescence, or a firmer age,
Affords a plea allowable or just

For making speech the pamperer of lust;
But when the breath of age commits the fault
'Tis nauseous as the vapour of a vault.
So wither'd stumps disgrace the sylvan scene,
No longer fruitful, and no longer green;
The sapless wood, divested of the bark,
Grows fungous, and takes fire at every spark.

Oaths terminate, as Paul observes, all strife—
Some men have surely then a peaceful life!
Whatever subject occupy discourse,
The feats of Vestris, or the naval force,
Asseveration blustering in your face
Makes contradiction such a hopeless case:
In every tale they tell, or false or true,
Well known, or such as no man ever knew,
They fix attention, heedless of your pain,
With oaths like rivets forced into the brain;
And e'en when sober truth prevails throughout,
They swear it, till affirmance breeds a doubt.
A Persian, humble servant of the sun,
Who, though devout, yet bigotry had none,
Hearing a lawyer, grave in his address,
With adjurations every word impress,
Supposed the man a bishop, or at least,
God's name so much upon his lips, a priest;
Bow'd at the close with all his graceful airs,
And begg'd an interest in his frequent prayers.

Go, quit the rank to which ye stood preferr'd,
Henceforth associate in one common herd;
Religion, virtue, reason, common sense,
Pronounce your human form a false pretence:
A mere disguise, in which a devil lurks,
Who yet betrays his secret by his works.

Ye powers who rule the tongue, if such there are,
And make colloquial happiness your care,
Preserve me from the thing I dread and hate,
A duel in the form of a debate.
The clash of arguments and jar of words,
Worse than the mortal brunt of rival swords,
Decide no question with their tedious length,
For opposition gives opinion strength,
Divert the champions prodigal of breath,
And put the peaceably disposed to death.
O thwart me not, Sir Soph, at every turn,
Nor carp at every flaw you may discern;
Though syllogisms hang not on my tongue,
I am not surely always in the wrong;
'Tis hard if all is false that I advance,

A fool must now and then be right by chance.
Not that all freedom of dissent I blame;
No—there I grant the privilege I claim.
A disputable point is no man's ground;
Rove where you please, 'tis common all around.
Discourse may want an animated—No,
To brush the surface, and to make it flow;
But still remember, if you mean to please,
To press your point with modesty and ease.
The mark, at which my juster aim I take,
Is contradiction for its own dear sake.
Set your opinion at whatever pitch,
Knots and impediments make something hitch;
Adopt his own, 'tis equally in vain,
Your thread of argument is snapp'd again;
The wrangler, rather than accord with you,
Will judge himself deceived, and prove it too.
Vociferated logic kills me quite,
A noisy man is always in the right,
I twirl my thumbs, fall back into my chair,
Fix on the wainscot a distressful stare,
And, when I hope his blunders are all out,
Reply discreetly—To be sure—no doubt!
    Dubius is such a scrupulous good man—
Yes—you may catch him tripping, if you can.
He would not, with a peremptory tone,
Assert the nose upon his face his own;
With hesitation admirably slow,
He humbly hopes—presumes—it may be so.
His evidence, if he were call'd by law
To swear to some enormity he saw,
For want of prominence and just relief,
Would hang an honest man and save a thief.
Through constant dread of giving truth offence,
He ties up all his hearers in suspense;
Knows what he knows as if he knew it not;
What he remembers seems to have forgot;
His sole opinion, whatsoe'er befall,
Centring at last in having none at all.
Yet, though he tease and balk your listening ear,
He makes one useful point exceeding clear;
Howe'er ingenious on his darling theme
A sceptic in philosophy may seem,
Reduced to practice, his beloved rule
Would only prove him a consummate fool;
Useless in him alike both brain and speech,
Fate having placed all truth above his reach,
His ambiguities his total sum,

He might as well be blind, and deaf, and dumb.
  Where men of judgment creep and feel their way,
The positive pronounce without dismay;
Their want of light and intellect supplied
By sparks absurdity strikes out of pride.
Without the means of knowing right from wrong,
They always are decisive, clear, and strong.
Where others toil with philosophic force,
Their nimble nonsense takes a shorter course;
Flings at your head conviction in the lump,
And gains remote conclusions at a jump:
Their own defect, invisible to them,
Seen in another, they at once condemn;
And, though self-idolised in every case,
Hate their own likeness in a brother's face.
The cause is plain, and not to be denied,
The proud are always most provoked by pride.
Few competitions but engender spite;
And those the most, where neither has a right.
  The point of honour has been deem'd of use,
To teach good manners, and to curb abuse:
Admit it true, the consequence is clear,
Our polish'd manners are a mask we wear,
And at the bottom barbarous still and rude;
We are restrain'd indeed, but not subdued.
The very remedy, however sure,
Springs from the mischief it intends to cure,
And savage in its principle appears,
Tried, as it should be, by the fruit it bears.
'Tis hard, indeed, if nothing will defend
Mankind from quarrels but their fatal end;
That now and then a hero must decease,
That the surviving world may live in peace.
Perhaps at last close scrutiny may show
The practice dastardly, and mean, and low;
That men engage in it compell'd by force;
And fear, not courage, is its proper source.
The fear of tyrant custom, and the fear
Lest fops should censure us, and fools should sneer.
At least to trample on our Maker's laws,
And hazard life for any or no cause,
To rush into a fix'd eternal state
Out of the very flames of rage and hate,
Or send another shivering to the bar
With all the guilt of such unnatural war,
Whatever use may urge, or honour plead,
On reason's verdict is a madman's deed.
Am I to set my life upon a throw,

Because a bear is rude and surly? No—
A moral, sensible, and well-bred man
Will not affront me, and no other can.
Were I empower'd to regulate the lists,
They should encounter with well loaded fists;
A Trojan combat would be something new,
Let Dares beat Entellus black and blue;
Then each might show, to his admiring friends,
In honourable bumps his rich amends,
And carry, in contusions of his skull,
A satisfactory receipt in full.
   A story, in which native humour reigns,
Is often useful, always entertains:
A graver fact, enlisted on your side,
May furnish illustration, well applied;
But sedentary weavers of long tales
Give me the fidgets, and my patience fails.
'Tis the most asinine employ on earth,
To hear them tell of parentage and birth,
And echo conversations dull and dry,
Embellish'd with—He said,—and, So said I.
At every interview their route the same,
The repetition makes attention lame:
We bustle up with unsuccessful speed,
And in the saddest part cry—Droll indeed!
The path of narrative with care pursue,
Still making probability your clue;
On all the vestiges of truth attend,
And let them guide you to a decent end.
Of all ambitious man may entertain,
The worst that can invade a sickly brain,
Is that which angles hourly for surprise,
And baits its hook with prodigies and lies.
Credulous infancy, or age as weak,
Are fittest auditors for such to seek,
Who to please others will themselves disgrace,
Yet please not, but affront you to your face,
A great retailer of this curious ware,
Having unloaded and made many stare,
Can this be true?—an arch observer cries;
Yes (rather moved), I saw it with these eyes!
Sir! I believe it on that ground alone;
I could not, had I seen it with my own.
   A tale should be judicious, clear, succinct;
The language plain, the incidents well linked;
Tell not as new what everybody knows,
And, new or old, still hasten to a close;
There, centring in a focus round and neat,

Let all your rays of information meet.
What neither yields us profit nor delight
Is like a nurse's lullaby at night;
Guy Earl of Warwick and fair Eleanore,
Or giant-killing Jack, would please me more.
   The pipe, with solemn interposing puff,
Makes half a sentence at a time enough;
The dozing sages drop the drowsy strain,
Then pause, and puff—and speak, and pause again.
Such often, like the tube they so admire,
Important triflers! have more smoke than fire.
Pernicious weed! whose scent the fair annoys,
Unfriendly to society's chief joys,
Thy worst effect is banishing for hours
The sex whose presence civilizes ours;
Thou art indeed the drug a gardener wants
To poison vermin that infest his plants;
But are we so to wit and beauty blind,
As to despise the glory of our kind,
And show the softest minds and fairest forms
As little mercy as he grubs and worms?
They dare not wait the riotous abuse
Thy thirst-creating steams at length produce,
When wine has given indecent language birth,
And forced the floodgates of licentious mirth;
For seaborn Venus her attachment shows
Still to that element from which she rose,
And, with a quiet which no fumes disturb,
Sips meek infusions of a milder herb.
   The emphatic speaker dearly loves to oppose,
In contact inconvenient, nose to nose,
As if the gnomon on his neighbour's phiz,
Touch'd with the magnet, had attracted his.
His whisper'd theme, dilated and at large,
Proves after all a wind-gun's airy charge,
An extract of his diary—no more,
A tasteless journal of the day before.
He walk'd abroad, o'ertaken in the rain,
Call'd on a friend, drank tea, stepp'd home again,
Resumed his purpose, had a world of talk
With one he stumbled on, and lost his walk.
I interrupt him with a sudden bow,
Adieu, dear sir! lest you should lose it now.
   I cannot talk with civet in the room,
A fine puss gentleman that's all perfume;
The sight's enough—no need to smell a beau—
Who thrusts his head into a raree-show?
His odoriferous attempts to please

Perhaps might prosper with a swarm of bees;
But we that make no honey, though we sting,
Poets, are sometimes apt to maul the thing.
'Tis wrong to bring into a mixed resort,
What makes some sick, and others à-la-mort,
An argument of cogence, we may say,
Why such a one should keep himself away.

   A graver coxcomb we may sometimes see,
Quite as absurd, though not so light as he:
A shallow brain behind a serious mask,
An oracle within an empty cask,
The solemn fop; significant and budge;
A fool with judges, amongst fools a judge.
He says but little, and that little said
Owes all its weight, like loaded dice, to lead.
His wit invites you by his looks to come,
But when you knock it never is at home:
'Tis like a parcel sent you by the stage,
Some handsome present, as your hopes presage;
'Tis heavy, bulky, and bids fair to prove
An absent friend's fidelity and love,
But when unpack'd your disappointment groans
To find it stuff'd with brickbats, earth, and stones.

   Some men employ their health, an ugly trick,
In making known how oft they have been sick,
And give us, in recitals of disease,
A doctor's trouble, but without the fees;
Relate how many weeks they kept their bed,
How an emetic or cathartic sped;
Nothing is slightly touch'd, much less forgot,
Nose, ears and eyes, seem present on the spot.
Now the distemper, spite of draught or pill,
Victorious seemed, and now the doctor's skill;
And now—alas for unforeseen mishaps!
They put on a damp nightcap and relapse;
They thought they must have died, they were so bad:
Their peevish hearers almost wish they had.

   Some fretful tempers wince at every touch,
You always do too little or too much:
You speak with life, in hopes to entertain,
Your elevated voice goes through the brain;
You fall at once into a lower key,
That's worse—the drone-pipe of an humble bee.
The southern sash admits too strong a light,
You rise and drop the curtain—now 'tis night.
He shakes with cold—you stir the fire and strive
To make a blaze—that's roasting him alive.
Serve him with venison, and he wishes fish;

With sole—that's just the sort he would not wish.
He takes what he at first professed to loathe,
And in due time feeds heartily on both;
Yet still, o'erclouded with a constant frown,
He does not swallow, but he gulps it down.
Your hope to please him vain on every plan,
Himself should work that wonder if he can—
Alas! his efforts double his distress,
He likes yours little, and his own still less.
Thus always teasing others, always teased,
His only pleasure is to be displeased.
  I pity bashful men, who feel the pain
Of fancied scorn and undeserved disdain,
And bear the marks upon a blushing face
Of needless shame and self-imposed disgrace.
Our sensibilities are so acute,
The fear of being silent makes us mute.
We sometimes think we could a speech produce
Much to the purpose, if our tongues were loose;
But, being tried, it dies upon the lip,
Faint as a chicken's note that has the pip:
Our wasted oil unprofitably burns,
Like hidden lamps in old sepulchral urns.
Few Frenchmen of this evil have complain'd;
It seems as if we Britons were ordained,
By way of wholesome curb upon our pride,
To fear each other, fearing none beside.
The cause perhaps inquiry may descry,
Self-searching with an introverted eye,
Conceal'd within an unsuspected part
The vainest corner of our own vain heart:
For ever aiming at the world's esteem,
Our self-importance ruins its own scheme;
In other eyes our talents rarely shown,
Become at length so splendid in our own,
We dare not risk them into public view,
Lest they miscarry of what seems their due.
True modesty is a discerning grace,
And only blushes in the proper place;
But counterfeit is blind, and skulks through fear,
Where 'tis a shame to be ashamed to appear:
Humility the parent of the first,
The last by vanity produced and nursed.
The circle form'd, we sit in silent state,
Like figures drawn upon a dial-plate;
Yes, ma'am, and No, ma'am, utter'd softly, show
Every five minutes how the minutes go;
Each individual, suffering a constraint

Poetry may, but colours cannot, paint;
And, if in close committee on the sky,
Reports it hot or cold, or wet or dry;
And finds a changing clime a happy source
Of wise reflection and well-timed discourse.
We next inquire, but softly and by stealth,
Like conservators of the public health,
Of epidemic throats, if such there are,
And coughs, and rheums, and phthisic, and catarrh.
That theme exhausted, a wide chasm ensues,
Fill'd up at last with interesting news,
Who danc'd with whom, and who are like to wed,
And who is hang'd, and who is brought to bed:
But fear to call a more important cause,
As if 'twere treason against English laws.
The visit paid, with ecstacy we come,
As from a seven years' transportation, home,
And there resume an unembarrass'd brow,
Recovering what we lost, we know not how,
The faculties that seem'd reduced to nought,
Expression and the privilege of thought.
   The reeking, roaring hero of the chase,
I give him over as a desperate case.
Physicians write in hopes to work a cure,
Never, if honest ones, when death is sure;
And though the fox he follows may be tamed,
A mere fox-follower never is reclaim'd.
Some farrier should prescribe his proper course,
Whose only fit companion is his horse,
Or if, deserving of a better doom,
The noble beast judge otherwise, his groom.
Yet e'en the rogue that serves him, though he stand
To take his honour's orders, cap in hand,
Prefers his fellow grooms with much good sense,
Their skill a truth, his master's a pretence.
If neither horse nor groom affect the 'squire,
Where can at last his jockeyship retire?
Oh, to the club, the scene of savage joys,
The school of coarse good fellowship and noise;
There, in the sweet society of those
Whose friendship from his boyish years he chose,
Let him improve his talent if he can,
Till none but beasts acknowledge him a man.
   Man's heart had been impenetrably seal'd,
Like theirs that cleave the flood or graze the field,
Had not his Maker's all-bestowing hand
Given him a soul, and bade him understand;
The reasoning power vouchsafed, of course inferr'd

The power to clothe that reason with his word;
For all is perfect that God works on earth,
And he that gives conception aids the birth.
If this be plain, 'tis plainly understood,
What uses of his boon the Giver would.
The mind despatch'd upon her busy toil,
Should range where Providence has bless'd the soil;
Visiting every flower with labour meet,
And gathering all her treasures sweet by sweet,
She should imbue the tongue with what she sips,
And shed the balmy blessing on the lips,
That good diffused may more abundant grow,
And speech may praise the power that bids it flow.
Will the sweet warbler of the livelong night,
That fills the listening lover with delight,
Forget his harmony, with rapture heard,
To learn the twittering of a meaner bird?
Or make the parrot's mimicry his choice,
That odious libel on a human voice?
No—nature, unsophisticate by man,
Starts not aside from her Creator's plan;
The melody, that was at first design'd
To cheer the rude forefathers of mankind,
Is note for note delivered in our ears,
In the last scene of her six thousand years.
Yet Fashion, leader of a chattering train,
Whom man, for his own hurt, permits to reign,
Who shifts and changes all things but his shape,
And would degrade her votary to an ape,
The fruitful parent of abuse and wrong,
Holds a usurp'd dominion o'er his tongue;
There sits and prompts him with his own disgrace,
Prescribes the theme, the tone, and the grimace,
And, when accomplish'd in her wayward school,
Calls gentleman whom she has made a fool.
'Tis an unalterable fix'd decree,
That none could frame or ratify but she,
That heaven and hell, and righteousness and sin,
Snares in his path, and foes that lurk within,
God and his attributes, (a field of day
Where 'tis an angel's happiness to stray,)
Fruits of his love and wonders of his might,
Be never named in ears esteem'd polite;
That he who dares, when she forbids, be grave,
Shall stand proscribed, a madman or a knave,
A close designer not to be believed,
Or, if excused that charge, at least deceived.
Oh folly worthy of the nurse's lap,

Give it the breast, or stop its mouth with pap!
Is it incredible, or can it seem
A dream to any except those that dream,
That man should love his Maker, and that fire,
Warming his heart, should at his lips transpire?
Know then, and modestly let fall your eyes,
And veil your daring crest that braves the skies;
That air of insolence affronts your God,
You need his pardon, and provoke his rod:
Now, in a posture that becomes you more
Than that heroic strut assumed before,
Know, your arrears with every hour accrue
For mercy shown, while wrath is justly due.
The time is short, and there are souls on earth,
Though future pain may serve for present mirth,
Acquainted with the woes that fear or shame,
By fashion taught, forbade them once to name,
And, having felt the pangs you deem a jest,
Have proved them truths too big to be express'd.
Go seek on revelation's hallow'd ground,
Sure to succeed, the remedy they found;
Touched by that power that you have dared to mock,
That makes seas stable, and dissolves the rock,
Your heart shall yield a life-renewing stream,
That fools, as you have done, shall call a dream.
  It happen'd on a solemn eventide,
Soon after He that was our surety died,
Two bosom friends, each pensively inclined,
The scene of all those sorrows left behind,
Sought their own village, busied as they went
In musings worthy of the great event:
They spake of him they loved, of him whose life,
Though blameless, had incurr'd perpetual strife,
Whose deeds had left, in spite of hostile arts,
A deep memorial graven on their hearts.
The recollection, like a vein of ore,
The farther traced, enrich'd them still the more;
They thought him, and they justly thought him, one
Sent to do more than he appear'd to have done;
To exalt a people, and to place them high
Above all else, and wonder'd he should die.
Ere yet they brought their journey to an end,
A stranger join'd them, courteous as a friend,
And ask'd them, with a kind engaging air,
What their affliction was, and begg'd a share.
Inform'd, he gather'd up the broken thread,
And, truth and wisdom gracing all he said,
Explain'd, illustrated, and search'd so well

The tender theme on which they chose to dwell,
That, reaching home, the night, they said, is near,
We must not now be parted, sojourn here—
The new acquaintance soon became a guest,
And made so welcome at their simple feast,
He bless'd the bread, but vanish'd at the word,
And left them both exclaiming, 'Twas the Lord!
Did not our hearts feel all he deign'd to say,
Did they not burn within us by the way?
  Now theirs was converse, such as it behoves
Man to maintain, and such as God approves:
Their views indeed were indistinct and dim,
But yet successful, being aim'd at him.
Christ and his character their only scope,
Their object, and their subject, and their hope,
They felt what it became them much to feel,
And, wanting him to loose the sacred seal,
Found him as prompt as their desire was true,
To spread the new-born glories in their view.
Well—what are ages and the lapse of time
Match'd against truths, as lasting as sublime?
Can length of years on God himself exact?
Or make that fiction which was once a fact?
No—marble and recording brass decay,
And, like the graver's memory, pass away;
The works of man inherit, as is just,
Their author's frailty, and return to dust:
But truth divine for ever stands secure,
Its head is guarded as its base is sure;
Fix'd in the rolling flood of endless years,
The pillar of the eternal plan appears,
The raving storm and dashing wave defies,
Built by that Architect who built the skies.
Hearts may be found, that harbour at this hour
That love of Christ, and all its quickening power;
And lips unstained by folly or by strife,
Whose wisdom, drawn from the deep well of life,
Tastes of its healthful origin, and flows
A Jordan for the ablution of our woes.
O days of heaven, and nights of equal praise,
Serene and peaceful as those heavenly days,
When souls drawn upwards in communion sweet
Enjoy the stillness of some close retreat,
Discourse, as if released and safe at home,
Of dangers past, and wonders yet to come,
And spread the sacred treasures of the breast
Upon the lap of covenanted rest!
  What, always dreaming over heavenly things,

Like angel-heads in stone with pigeon-wings?
Canting and whining out all day the word,
And half the night? fanatic and absurd!
Mine be the friend less frequent in his prayers,
Who makes no bustle with his soul's affairs,
Whose wit can brighten up a wint'ry day,
And chase the splenetic dull hours away;
Content on earth in earthly things to shine,
Who waits for heaven ere he becomes divine,
Leaves saints to enjoy those altitudes they teach,
And plucks the fruit placed more within his reach.
　Well spoken, advocate of sin and shame,
Known by thy bleating, Ignorance thy name.
Is sparkling wit the world's exclusive right?
The fix'd fee-simple of the vain and light?
Can hopes of heaven, bright prospects of an hour,
That come to waft us out of sorrow's power,
Obscure or quench a faculty that finds
Its happiest soil in the serenest minds?
Religion curbs indeed its wanton play,
And brings the trifler under rigorous sway,
But gives it usefulness unknown before,
And purifying, makes it shine the more.
A Christian's wit is inoffensive light,
A beam that aids, but never grieves the sight;
Vigorous in age as in the flush of youth;
'Tis always active on the side of truth;
Temperance and peace ensure its healthful state,
And make it brightest at its latest date.
Oh I have seen (nor hope perhaps in vain,
Ere life go down, to see such sights again)
A veteran warrior in the Christian field,
Who never saw the sword he could not wield;
Grave without dulness, learned without pride,
Exact, yet not precise, though meek, keen-eyed;
A man that would have foil'd at their own play
A dozen would-be's of the modern day;
Who, when occasion justified its use,
Had wit as bright as ready to produce,
Could fetch from records of an earlier age,
Or from philosophy's enlighten'd page,
His rich materials, and regale your ear
With strains it was a privilege to hear:
Yet above all his luxury supreme,
And his chief glory, was the gospel theme;
There he was copious as old Greece or Rome,
His happy eloquence seem'd there at home,
Ambitious not to shine or to excel,

But to treat justly what he loved so well.
    It moves me more perhaps than folly ought,
When some green heads, as void of wit as thought,
Suppose themselves monopolists of sense,
And wiser men's ability pretence.
Though time will wear us, and we must grow old,
Such men are not forgot as soon as cold,
Their fragrant memory will outlast their tomb,
Embalm'd for ever in its own perfume.
And to say truth, though in its early prime,
And when unstain'd with any grosser crime,
Youth has a sprightliness and fire to boast,
That in the valley of decline are lost,
And virtue with peculiar charms appears,
Crown'd with the garland of life's blooming years;
Yet age, by long experience well inform'd,
Well read, well temper'd, with religion warm'd,
That fire abated which impels rash youth,
Proud of his speed, to overshoot the truth,
As time improves the grape's authentic juice,
Mellows and makes the speech more fit for use,
And claims a reverence in its shortening day,
That 'tis an honour and a joy to pay.
The fruits of age, less fair, are yet more sound,
Than those a brighter season pours around;
And, like the stores autumnal suns mature,
Through wintry rigours unimpair'd endure.
    What is fanatic frenzy, scorn'd so much,
And dreaded more than a contagious touch?
I grant it dangerous, and approve your fear,
That fire is catching, if you draw too near;
But sage observers oft mistake the flame,
And give true piety that odious name.
To tremble (as the creature of an hour
Ought at the view of an almighty power)
Before his presence, at whose awful throne
All tremble in all worlds, except our own,
To supplicate his mercy, love his ways,
And prize them above pleasure, wealth, or praise,
Though common sense, allow'd a casting voice,
And free from bias, must approve the choice,
Convicts a man fanatic in the extreme,
And wild as madness in the world's esteem.
But that disease, when soberly defined,
Is the false fire of an o'erheated mind;
It views the truth with a distorted eye,
And either warps or lays it useless by;
'Tis narrow, selfish, arrogant, and draws

Its sordid nourishment from man's applause;
And, while at heart sin unrelinquish'd lies,
Presumes itself chief favourite of the skies.
'Tis such a light as putrefaction breeds
In fly-blown flesh, whereon the maggot feeds,
Shines in the dark, but, usher'd into day,
The stench remains, the lustre dies away.
   True bliss, if man may reach it, is composed
Of hearts in union mutually disclosed;
And, farewell else all hope of pure delight,
Those hearts should be reclaim'd, renew'd, upright.
Bad men, profaning friendship's hallow'd name,
Form, in its stead, a covenant of shame.
A dark confederacy against the laws
Of virtue, and religion's glorious cause:
They build each other up with dreadful skill,
As bastions set point-blank against God's will;
Enlarge and fortify the dread redoubt,
Deeply resolved to shut a Saviour out;
Call legions up from hell to back the deed;
And, cursed with conquest, finally succeed.
But souls, that carry on a blest exchange
Of joys they meet with in their heavenly range,
And with a fearless confidence make known
The sorrows sympathy esteems its own,
Daily derive increasing light and force
From such communion in their pleasant course,
Feel less the journey's roughness and its length,
Meet their opposers with united strength,
And, one in heart, in interest, and design,
Gird up each other to the race divine.
   But Conversation, choose what theme we may,
And chiefly when religion leads the way,
Should flow, like waters after summer showers,
Not as if raised by mere mechanic powers.
The Christian, in whose soul, though now distress'd,
Lives the dear thought of joys he once possess'd,
When all his glowing language issued forth
With God's deep stamp upon its current worth,
Will speak without disguise, and must impart,
Sad as it is, his undissembling heart,
Abhors constraint, and dares not feign a zeal,
Or seem to boast a fire, he does not feel.
The song of Sion is a tasteless thing,
Unless, when rising on a joyful wing,
The soul can mix with the celestial bands,
And give the strain the compass it demands.
   Strange tidings these to tell a world, who treat

All but their own experience as deceit!
Will they believe, though credulous enough
To swallow much upon much weaker proof,
That there are blest inhabitants of earth,
Partakers of a new ethereal birth,
Their hopes, desires, and purposes estranged
From things terrestrial, and divinely changed,
Their very language of a kind that speaks
The soul's sure interest in the good she seeks,
Who deal with scripture, its importance felt,
As Tully with philosophy once dealt,
And, in the silent watches of the night,
And through the scenes of toil-renewing light,
The social walk, or solitary ride,
Keep still the dear companion at their side?
No—shame upon a self-disgracing age,
God's work may serve an ape upon a stage
With such a jest as fill'd with hellish glee
Certain invisibles as shrewd as he;
But veneration or respect finds none,
Save from the subjects of that work alone.
The World grown old her deep discernment shows,
Claps spectacles on her sagacious nose,
Peruses closely the true Christian's face,
And finds it a mere mask of sly grimace;
Usurps God's office, lays his bosom bare,
And finds hypocrisy close lurking there;
And, serving God herself through mere constraint,
Concludes his unfeign'd love of him a feint.
And yet, God knows, look human nature through,
(And in due time the world shall know it too)
That since the flowers of Eden felt the blast,
That after man's defection laid all waste,
Sincerity towards the heart-searching God
Has made the new-born creature her abode,
Nor shall be found in unregenerate souls
Till the last fire burn all between the poles.
Sincerity! why 'tis his only pride,
Weak and imperfect in all grace beside,
He knows that God demands his heart entire,
And gives him all his just demands require.
Without it, his pretensions were as vain
As, having it, he deems the world's disdain;
That great defect would cost him not alone
Man's favourable judgment but his own;
His birthright shaken, and no longer clear
Than while his conduct proves his heart sincere.
Retort the charge, and let the world be told

She boasts a confidence she does not hold;
That, conscious of her crimes, she feels instead
A cold misgiving and a killing dread:
That while in health the ground of her support
Is madly to forget that life is short;
That sick she trembles, knowing she must die,
Her hope presumption, and her faith a lie;
That while she dotes and dreams that she believes,
She mocks her Maker, and herself deceives,
Her utmost reach, historical assent,
The doctrines warp'd to what they never meant;
That truth itself is in her head as dull
And useless as a candle in a skull,
And all her love of God a groundless claim,
A trick upon the canvas, painted flame.
Tell her again, the sneer upon her face,
And all her censures of the work of grace,
Are insincere, meant only to conceal
A dread she would not, yet is forced to feel;
That in her heart the Christian she reveres,
And, while she seems to scorn him, only fears.
  A poet does not work by square or line,
As smiths and joiners perfect a design;
At least we moderns, our attention less,
Beyond the example of our sires digress,
And claim a right to scamper and run wide,
Wherever chance, caprice, or fancy guide.
The world and I fortuitously met;
I owed a trifle, and have paid the debt;
She did me wrong, I recompensed the deed,
And, having struck the balance, now proceed.
Perhaps, however, as some years have pass'd
Since she and I conversed together last,
And I have lived recluse in rural shades,
Which seldom a distinct report pervades,
Great changes and new manners have occurr'd,
And blest reforms that I have never heard,
And she may now be as discreet and wise,
As once absurd in all discerning eyes.
Sobriety perhaps may now be found
Where once intoxication press'd the ground;
The subtle and injurious may be just,
And he grown chaste that was the slave of lust;
Arts once esteem'd may be with shame dismiss'd;
Charity may relax the miser's fist;
The gamester may have cast his cards away,
Forgot to curse, and only kneel to pray.
It has indeed been told me (with what weight,

How credibly, 'tis hard for me to state,)
That fables old, that seem'd for ever mute,
Revived, are hastening into fresh repute,
And gods and goddesses, discarded long,
Like useless lumber or a stroller's song,
Are bringing into vogue their heathen train,
And Jupiter bids fair to rule again;
That certain feasts are instituted now,
Where Venus hears the lover's tender vow;
That all Olympus through the country roves,
To consecrate our few remaining groves,
And Echo learns politely to repeat
The praise of names for ages obsolete;
That having proved the weakness, it should seem,
Of revelation's ineffectual beam,
To bring the passions under sober sway,
And give the moral springs their proper play,
They mean to try what may at last be done,
By stout substantial gods of wood and stone,
And whether Roman rites may not produce
The virtues of old Rome for English use.
May such success attend the pious plan,
May Mercury once more embellish man,
Grace him again with long forgotten arts,
Reclaim his taste, and brighten up his parts,
Make him athletic as in days of old,
Learn'd at the bar, in the palæstra bold,
Divest the rougher sex of female airs,
And teach the softer not to copy theirs:
The change shall please, nor shall it matter aught,
Who works the wonder, if it be but wrought.
'Tis time, however, if the case stands thus,
For us plain folks, and all who side with us,
To build our altar, confident and bold,
And say, as stern Elijah said of old,
The strife now stands upon a fair award,
If Israel's Lord be God, then serve the Lord:
If he be silent, faith is all a whim,
Then Baal is the God, and worship him.

  Digression is so much in modern use,
Thought is so rare, and fancy so profuse,
Some never seem so wide of their intent,
As when returning to the theme they meant;
As mendicants, whose business is to roam,
Make every parish but their own their home.
Though such continual zigzags in a book,
Such drunken reelings have an awkward look,
And I had rather creep to what is true,

Than rove and stagger with no mark in view;
Yet to consult a little, seem'd no crime,
The freakish humour of the present time:
But now to gather up what seems dispersed,
And touch the subject I design'd at first,
May prove, though much beside the rules of art,
Best for the public, and my wisest part.
And first, let no man charge me, that I mean
To clothe in sable every social scene,
And give good company a face severe,
As if they met around a father's bier;
For tell some men that, pleasure all their bent,
And laughter all their work, is life misspent,
Their wisdom bursts into this sage reply,
Then mirth is sin, and we should always cry.
To find the medium asks some share of wit,
And therefore 'tis a mark fools never hit.
But though life's valley be a vale of tears,
A brighter scene beyond that vale appears,
Whose glory, with a light that never fades,
Shoots between scatter'd rocks and opening shades,
And, while it shows the land the soul desires,
The language of the land she seeks inspires.
Thus touch'd, the tongue receives a sacred cure
Of all that was absurd, profane, impure;
Held within modest bounds, the tide of speech
Pursues the course that truth and nature teach;
No longer labours merely to produce
The pomp of sound, or tinkle without use:
Where'er it winds, the salutary stream,
Sprightly and fresh, enriches every theme,
While all the happy man possess'd before,
The gift of nature, or the classic store,
Is made subservient to the grand design,
For which Heaven form'd the faculty divine.
So, should an idiot, while at large he strays,
Find the sweet lyre on which an artist plays,
With rash and awkward force the chords he shakes,
And grins with wonder at the jar he makes;
But let the wise and well-instructed hand
Once take the shell beneath his just command,
In gentle sounds it seems as it complain'd
Of the rude injuries it late sustain'd,
Till, tuned at length to some immortal song,
It sounds Jehovah's name, and pours his praise along.

...... studiis florens ignobilis otî.
Virg. Georg. lib. iv.

The busy universally desirous of retirement—Important purpose for which this desire was given to man—
Musing on the works of the creation, a happy employment—The service of God not incompatible,
however, with a life of business—Human life; its pursuits—Various motives for seeking retirement—The
poet's delight in the study of nature—The lover's fondness for retirement—The hypochondriac—
Melancholy, a malady that claims most compassion, receives the least—Sufferings of the melancholy
man—The statesman's retirement—His new mode of life and company—Soon weary of retirement, he
returns to his former pursuits—Citizens' villas—Fashion of frequenting watering-places—The ocean—The
spendthrift in forced retirement—The sportsman ostler—The management of leisure a difficult task—
Man will be summoned to account for the employment of life—Books and friends requisite for the man
of leisure; and divine communion to fill the remaining void—Religion not adverse to innocent pleasures—
The poet concludes with reference to his own pursuit.

Hackney'd in business, wearied at that oar,
Which thousands, once fast chain'd to, quit no more,
But which, when life at ebb runs weak and low,
All wish, or seem to wish, they could forego;
The statesman, lawyer, merchant, man of trade,
Pants for the refuge of some rural shade,
Where, all his long anxieties forgot
Amid the charms of a sequester'd spot,
Or recollected only to gild o'er,
And add a smile to what was sweet before,
He may possess the joys he thinks he sees,
Lay his old age upon the lap of ease,
Improve the remnant of his wasted span,
And, having lived a trifler, die a man.
Thus conscience pleads her cause within the breast,
Though long rebell'd against, not yet suppress'd,
And calls a creature form'd for God alone,
For Heaven's high purposes, and not his own,
Calls him away from selfish ends and aims,
From what debilitates and what inflames,
From cities humming with a restless crowd,
Sordid as active, ignorant as loud,
Whose highest praise is that they live in vain,
The dupes of pleasure, or the slaves of gain,
Where works of man are cluster'd close around,
And works of God are hardly to be found,
To regions where, in spite of sin and woe,
Traces of Eden are still seen below,
Where mountain, river, forest, field, and grove,

Remind him of his Maker's power and love.
'Tis well if, look'd for at so late a day,
In the last scene of such a senseless play,
True wisdom will attend his feeble call,
And grace his action ere the curtain fall.
Souls, that have long despised their heavenly birth,
Their wishes all impregnated with earth,
For threescore years employ'd with ceaseless care
In catching smoke and feeding upon air,
Conversant only with the ways of men,
Rarely redeem the short remaining ten.
Inveterate habits choke the unfruitful heart,
Their fibres penetrate its tenderest part,
And, draining its nutritious powers to feed
Their noxious growth, starve every better seed.
  Happy, if full of days—but happier far,
If, ere we yet discern life's evening star,
Sick of the service of a world, that feeds
Its patient drudges with dry chaff and weeds,
We can escape from custom's idiot sway,
To serve the sovereign we were born to obey.
Then sweet to muse upon his skill display'd
(Infinite skill) in all that he has made!
To trace in nature's most minute design
The signature and stamp of power divine,
Contrivance intricate, express'd with ease,
Where unassisted sight no beauty sees,
The shapely limb and lubricated joint,
Within the small dimensions of a point,
Muscle and nerve miraculously spun,
His mighty work, who speaks and it is done,
The invisible in things scarce seen reveal'd,
To whom an atom is an ample field:
To wonder at a thousand insect forms,
These hatch'd, and those resuscitated worms,
New life ordain'd and brighter scenes to share,
Once prone on earth, now buoyant upon air,
Whose shape would make them, had they bulk and size,
More hideous foes than fancy can devise;
With helmet-heads and dragon-scales adorn'd,
The mighty myriads, now securely scorn'd,
Would mock the majesty of man's high birth,
Despise his bulwarks, and unpeople earth:
Then with a glance of fancy to survey,
Far as the faculty can stretch away,
Ten thousand rivers pour'd at his command,
From urns that never fail, through every land;
These like a deluge with impetuous force,

Those winding modestly a silent course;
The cloud-surmounting Alps, the fruitful vales;
Seas, on which every nation spreads her sails;
The sun, a world whence other worlds drink light,
The crescent moon, the diadem of night:
Stars countless, each in his appointed place,
Fast anchor'd in the deep abyss of space—
At such a sight to catch the poet's flame,
And with a rapture like his own exclaim
These are thy glorious works, thou Source of Good,
How dimly seen, how faintly understood!
Thine, and upheld by thy paternal care,
This universal frame, thus wondrous fair;
Thy power divine, and bounty beyond thought,
Adored and praised in all that thou hast wrought.
Absorbed in that immensity I see,
I shrink abased, and yet aspire to thee;
Instruct me, guide me to that heavenly day
Thy words more clearly than thy works display,
That, while thy truths my grosser thoughts refine,
I may resemble thee, and call thee mine.
    O blest proficiency! surpassing all
That men erroneously their glory call,
The recompence that arts or arms can yield,
The bar, the senate, or the tented field.
Compared with this sublimest life below,
Ye kings and rulers, what have courts to show?
Thus studied, used, and consecrated thus,
On earth what is, seems form'd indeed for us;
Not as the plaything of a froward child,
Fretful unless diverted and beguiled,
Much less to feed and fan the fatal fires
Of pride, ambition, or impure desires,
But as a scale, by which the soul ascends
From mighty means to more important ends,
Securely, though by steps but rarely trod,
Mounts from inferior beings up to God,
And sees, by no fallacious light or dim,
Earth made for man, and man himself for him.
    Not that I mean to approve, or would enforce,
A superstitious and monastic course:
Truth is not local, God alike pervades
And fills the world of traffic and the shades,
And may be fear'd amidst the busiest scenes,
Or scorn'd where business never intervenes.
But, 'tis not easy with a mind like ours,
Conscious of weakness in its noblest powers,
And in a world where, other ills apart,

The roving eye misleads the careless heart,
To limit thought, by nature prone to stray
Wherever freakish fancy points the way;
To bid the pleadings of self-love be still,
Resign our own and seek our Maker's will;
To spread the page of scripture, and compare
Our conduct with the laws engraven there;
To measure all that passes in the breast,
Faithfully, fairly, by that sacred test;
To dive into the secret deeps within,
To spare no passion and no favourite sin,
And search the themes, important above all,
Ourselves, and our recovery from our fall.
But leisure, silence, and a mind released
From anxious thoughts how wealth may be increased,
How to secure, in some propitious hour,
The point of interest or the post of power,
A soul serene, and equally retired
From objects too much dreaded or desired,
Safe from the clamours of perverse dispute,
At least are friendly to the great pursuit.
   Opening the map of God's extensive plan,
We find a little isle, this life of man;
Eternity's unknown expanse appears
Circling around and limiting his years.
The busy race examine and explore
Each creek and cavern of the dangerous shore,
With care collect what in their eyes excels,
Some shining pebbles, and some weeds and shells,
Thus laden, dream that they are rich and great,
And happiest he that groans beneath his weight.
The waves o'ertake them in their serious play,
And every hour sweeps multitudes away;
They shriek and sink, survivors start and weep,
Pursue their sport, and follow to the deep.
A few forsake the throng; with lifted eyes
Ask wealth of Heaven, and gain a real prize,
Truth, wisdom, grace, and peace like that above,
Seal'd with his signet, whom they serve and love;
Scorn'd by the rest, with patient hope they wait
A kind release from their imperfect state,
And unregretted are soon snatch'd away
From scenes of sorrow into glorious day.
   Nor these alone prefer a life recluse,
Who seek retirement for its proper use;
The love of change, that lives in every breast,
Genius, and temper, and desire of rest,
Discordant motives in one centre meet,

And each inclines its votary to retreat.
Some minds by nature are averse to noise,
And hate the tumult half the world enjoys,
The lure of avarice, or the pompous prize
That courts display before ambitious eyes;
The fruits that hang on pleasure's flowery stem,
Whate'er enchants them, are no snares to them.
To them the deep recess of dusky groves,
Or forest, where the deer securely roves,
The fall of waters, and the song of birds,
And hills that echo to the distant herds,
Are luxuries excelling all the glare
The world can boast, and her chief favourites share.
With eager step, and carelessly array'd,
For such a cause the poet seeks the shade,
From all he sees he catches new delight,
Pleased Fancy claps her pinions at the sight,
The rising or the setting orb of day,
The clouds that flit, or slowly float away,
Nature in all the various shapes she wears,
Frowning in storms, or breathing gentle airs,
The snowy robe her wintry state assumes,
Her summer heats, her fruits, and her perfumes,
All, all alike transport the glowing bard,
Success in rhyme his glory and reward.
O Nature! whose Elysian scenes disclose
His bright perfections at whose word they rose,
Next to that power who form'd thee, and sustains,
Be thou the great inspirer of my strains.
Still, as I touch the lyre, do thou expand
Thy genuine charms, and guide an artless hand,
That I may catch a fire but rarely known,
Give useful light, though I should miss renown,
And, poring on thy page, whose every line
Bears proof of an intelligence divine,
May feel a heart enrich'd by what it pays,
That builds its glory on its Maker's praise.
Woe to the man whose wit disclaims its use,
Glittering in vain, or only to seduce,
Who studies nature with a wanton eye,
Admires the work, but slips the lesson by;
His hours of leisure and recess employs
In drawing pictures of forbidden joys,
Retires to blazon his own worthless name,
Or shoot the careless with a surer aim.
  The lover too shuns business and alarms,
Tender idolater of absent charms.
Saints offer nothing in their warmest prayers

That he devotes not with a zeal like theirs;
'Tis consecration of his heart, soul, time,
And every thought that wanders is a crime.
In sighs he worships his supremely fair,
And weeps a sad libation in despair;
Adores a creature, and, devout in vain,
Wins in return an answer of disdain.
As woodbine weds the plant within her reach,
Rough elm, or smooth-grain'd ash, or glossy beech,
In spiral rings ascends the trunk, and lays
Her golden tassels on the leafy sprays,
But does a mischief while she lends a grace,
Straightening its growth by such a strict embrace;
So love, that clings around the noblest minds
Forbids the advancement of the soul he binds;
The suitor's air indeed he soon improves,
And forms it to the taste of her he loves,
Teaches his eyes a language, and no less
Refines his speech, and fashions his address;
But farewell promises of happier fruits,
Manly designs, and learning's grave pursuits;
Girt with a chain he cannot wish to break,
His only bliss is sorrow for her sake;
Who will may pant for glory and excel,
Her smile his aim, all higher aims farewell!
Thyrsis, Alexis, or whatever name
May least offend against so pure a flame,
Though sage advice of friends the most sincere
Sounds harshly in so delicate an ear,
And lovers, of all creatures, tame or wild,
Can least brook management, however mild,
Yet let a poet (poetry disarms
The fiercest animals with magic charms)
Risk an intrusion on thy pensive mood,
And woo and win thee to thy proper good.
Pastoral images and still retreats,
Umbrageous walks and solitary seats,
Sweet birds in concert with harmonious streams,
Soft airs, nocturnal vigils, and day-dreams,
Are all enchantments in a case like thine,
Conspire against thy peace with one design,
Soothe thee to make thee but a surer prey,
And feed the fire that wastes thy powers away.
Up—God has formed thee with a wiser view,
Not to be led in chains, but to subdue;
Calls thee to cope with enemies, and first
Points out a conflict with thyself, the worst.
Woman indeed, a gift he would bestow

When he design'd a Paradise below,
The richest earthly boon his hands afford,
Deserves to be beloved, but not adored.
Post away swiftly to more actives scenes,
Collect the scatter'd truth that study gleans,
Mix with the world, but with its wiser part,
No longer give an image all thine heart;
Its empire is not hers, nor is it thine,
'Tis God's just claim, prerogative divine.
  Virtuous and faithful Heberden, whose skill
Attempts no task it cannot well fulfil,
Gives melancholy up to nature's care,
And sends the patient into purer air.
Look were he comes—in this embower'd alcove
Stand close conceal'd, and see a statue move:
Lips busy, and eyes fix'd, foot falling slow,
Arms hanging idly down, hands clasp'd below,
Interpret to the marking eye distress,
Such as its symptoms can alone express.
That tongue is silent now; that silent tongue
Could argue once, could jest, or join the song,
Could give advice, could censure or commend,
Or charm the sorrows of a drooping friend.
Renounced alike its office and its sport,
Its brisker and its graver strains fall short;
Both fail beneath a fever's secret sway,
And like a summer-brook are past away.
This is a sight for pity to peruse,
Till she resemble faintly what she views,
Till sympathy contract a kindred pain,
Pierced with the woes that she laments in vain.
This, of all maladies that man infest,
Claims most compassion, and receives the least:
Job felt it, when he groan'd beneath the rod
And the barb'd arrows of a frowning God;
And such emollients as his friends could spare,
Friends such as his for modern Jobs prepare.
Blest, rather curst, with hearts that never feel,
Kept snug in caskets of close-hammer'd steel,
With mouths made only to grin wide and eat,
And minds that deem derided pain a treat,
With limbs of British oak, and nerves of wire,
And wit that puppet prompters might inspire,
Their sovereign nostrum is a clumsy joke
On pangs enforced with God's severest stroke.
But, with a soul that ever felt the sting
Of sorrow, sorrow is a sacred thing:
Not to molest, or irritate, or raise

A laugh at his expense, is slender praise;
He that has not usurp'd the name of man
Does all, and deems too little all, he can,
To assuage the throbbings of the fester'd part,
And staunch the bleedings of a broken heart.
'Tis not, as heads that never ache suppose,
Forgery of fancy, and a dream of woes;
Man is a harp, whose chords elude the sight,
Each yielding harmony disposed aright;
The screws reversed (a task which if he please
God in a moment executes with ease),
Ten thousand thousand strings at once go loose,
Lost, till he tune them, all their power and use.
Then neither heathy wilds, nor scenes as fair
As ever recompensed the peasant's care,
Nor soft declivities with tufted hills,
Nor view of waters turning busy mills,
Parks in which art preceptress nature weds,
Nor gardens interspersed with flowery beds,
Nor gales, that catch the scent of blooming groves,
And waft it to the mourner as he roves,
Can call up life into his faded eye,
That passes all he sees unheeded by;
No wounds like those a wounded spirit feels,
No cure for such, till God who makes them heals.
And thou, sad sufferer under nameless ill
That yields not to the touch of human skill,
Improve the kind occasion, understand
A Father's frown, and kiss his chastening hand.
To thee the day-spring, and the blaze of noon,
The purple evening and resplendent moon,
The stars that, sprinkled o'er the vault of night,
Seem drops descending in a shower of light,
Shine not, or undesired and hated shine,
Seen through the medium of a cloud like thine:
Yet seek him, in his favour life is found,
All bliss beside—a shadow or a sound:
Then heaven, eclipsed so long, and this dull earth,
Shall seem to start into a second birth;
Nature, assuming a more lovely face,
Borrowing a beauty from the works of grace,
Shall be despised and overlook'd no more,
Shall fill thee with delights unfelt before,
Impart to things inanimate a voice,
And bid her mountains and her hills rejoice;
The sound shall run along the winding vales,
And thou enjoy an Eden ere it fails.
    Ye groves, (the statesman at his desk exclaims,

Sick of a thousand disappointed aims,)
My patrimonial treasure and my pride,
Beneath your shades your grey possessor hide,
Receive me, languishing for that repose
The servant of the public never knows.
Ye saw me once (ah, those regretted days,
When boyish innocence was all my praise!)
Hour after hour delightfully allot
To studies then familiar, since forgot,
And cultivate a taste for ancient song,
Catching its ardour as I mused along;
Nor seldom, as propitious Heaven might send,
What once I valued and could boast, a friend,
Were witnesses how cordially I press'd
His undissembling virtue to my breast;
Receive me now, not uncorrupt as then
Nor guiltless of corrupting other men,
But versed in arts that, while they seem to stay
A falling empire, hasten its decay.
To the fair haven of my native home,
The wreck of what I was, fatigued, I come;
For once I can approve the patriot's voice,
And make the course he recommends my choice:
We meet at last in one sincere desire,
His wish and mine both prompt me to retire.
'Tis done—he steps into the welcome chaise,
Lolls at his ease behind four handsome bays,
That whirl away from business and debate
The disencumber'd Atlas of the state.
Ask not the boy, who, when the breeze of morn
First shakes the glittering drops from every thorn,
Unfolds his flock, then under bank or bush
Sits linking cherry-stones, or platting rush,
How fair is Freedom?—he was always free:
To carve his rustic name upon a tree,
To snare the mole, or with ill-fashion'd hook
To draw the incautious minnow from the brook,
Are life's prime pleasures in his simple view,
His flock the chief concern he ever knew;
She shines but little in his heedless eyes,
The good we never miss we rarely prize:
But ask the noble drudge in state affairs,
Escaped from office and its constant cares,
What charms he sees in Freedom's smile express'd,
In freedom lost so long, now repossess'd;
The tongue whose strains were cogent as commands,
Revered at home, and felt in foreign lands,
Shall own itself a stammerer in that cause,

Or plead its silence as its best applause.
He knows indeed that, whether dress'd or rude,
Wild without art, or artfully subdued,
Nature in every form inspires delight,
But never mark'd her with so just a sight.
Her hedge-row shrubs, a variegated store,
With woodbine and wild roses mantled o'er,
Green balks and furrow'd lands, the stream that spreads
Its cooling vapour o'er the dewy meads,
Downs, that almost escape the inquiring eye,
That melt and fade into the distant sky,
Beauties he lately slighted as he pass'd,
Seem all created since he travell'd last.
Master of all the enjoyments he design'd,
No rough annoyance rankling in his mind,
What early philosophic hours he keeps,
How regular his meals, how sound he sleeps!
Not sounder he that on the mainmast head,
While morning kindles with a windy red,
Begins a long look-out for distant land,
Nor quits till evening watch his giddy stand,
Then, swift descending with a seaman's haste,
Slips to his hammock, and forgets the blast.
He chooses company, but not the squire's,
Whose wit is rudeness, whose good breeding tires;
Nor yet the parson's, who would gladly come,
Obsequious when abroad, though proud at home;
Nor can he much affect the neighbouring peer,
Whose toe of emulation treads too near;
But wisely seeks a more convenient friend,
With whom, dismissing forms, he may unbend.
A man, whom marks of condescending grace
Teach, while they flatter him, his proper place;
Who comes when call'd, and at a word withdraws,
Speaks with reserve, and listens with applause;
Some plain mechanic, who, without pretence
To birth or wit, nor gives nor takes offence;
On whom he rests well pleased his weary powers,
And talks and laughs away his vacant hours.
The tide of life, swift always in its course,
May run in cities with a brisker force,
But no where with a current so serene,
Or half so clear, as in the rural scene.
Yet how fallacious is all earthly bliss,
What obvious truths the wisest heads may miss;
Some pleasures live a month, and some a year,
But short the date of all we gather here;
No happiness is felt, except the true,

That does not charm thee more for being new.
This observation, as it chanced, not made,
Or, if the thought occurr'd, not duly weigh'd,
He sighs—for after all by slow degrees
The spot he loved has lost the power to please;
To cross his ambling pony day by day
Seems at the best but dreaming life away;
The prospect, such as might enchant despair,
He views it not, or sees no beauty there;
With aching heart, and discontented looks,
Returns at noon to billiards or to books,
But feels, while grasping at his faded joys,
A secret thirst of his renounced employs.
He chides the tardiness of every post,
Pants to be told of battles won or lost,
Blames his own indolence, observes, though late,
'Tis criminal to leave a sinking state,
Flies to the levee, and, received with grace,
Kneels, kisses hands, and shines again in place.
   Suburban villas, highway-side retreats,
That dread the encroachment of our growing streets,
Tight boxes, neatly sash'd, and in a blaze
With all a July sun's collected rays,
Delight the citizen, who, gasping there,
Breathes clouds of dust, and calls it country air.
O sweet retirement, who would balk the thought
That could afford retirement, or could not?
'Tis such an easy walk, so smooth and straight,
The second milestone fronts the garden gate;
A step if fair, and, if a shower approach,
You find safe shelter in the next stage-coach.
There, prison'd in a parlour snug and small,
Like bottled wasps upon a southern wall,
The man of business and his friends compress'd
Forget their labours, and yet find no rest;
But still 'tis rural—trees are to be seen
From every window, and the fields are green;
Ducks paddle in the pond before the door,
And what could a remoter scene show more?
A sense of elegance we rarely find
The portion of a mean or vulgar mind,
And ignorance of better things makes man,
Who cannot much, rejoice in what he can;
And he, that deems his leisure well bestow'd
In contemplation of a turnpike-road,
Is occupied as well, employs his hours
As wisely, and as much improves his powers,
As he that slumbers in pavilions graced

With all the charms of an accomplish'd taste.
Yet hence, alas! insolvencies; and hence
The unpitied victim of ill-judged expense,
From all his wearisome engagements freed,
Shakes hands with business, and retires indeed.

   Your prudent grandmammas, ye modern belles,
Content with Bristol, Bath, and Tunbridge Wells,
When health required it, would consent to roam,
Else more attach'd to pleasures found at home;
But now alike, gay widow, virgin, wife,
Ingenious to diversify dull life,
In coaches, chaises, caravans, and hoys,
Fly to the coast for daily, nightly joys,
And all, impatient of dry land, agree
With one consent to rush into the sea.
Ocean exhibits, fathomless and broad,
Much of the power and majesty of God.
He swathes about the swelling of the deep,
That shines and rests, as infants smile and sleep;
Vast as it is, it answers as it flows
The breathings of the lightest air that blows;
Curling and whitening over all the waste,
The rising waves obey the increasing blast,
Abrupt and horrid as the tempest roars,
Thunder and flash upon the stedfast shores,
Till he that rides the whirlwind checks the rein,
Then all the world of waters sleeps again.
Nereids or Dryads, as the fashion leads,
Now in the floods, now panting in the meads,
Votaries of pleasure still, where'er she dwells,
Near barren rocks, in palaces, or cells,
O grant a poet leave to recommend
(A poet fond of nature, and your friend)
Her slighted works to your admiring view;
Her works must needs excel, who fashion'd you.
Would ye, when rambling in your morning ride,
With some unmeaning coxcomb at your side,
Condemn the prattler for his idle pains,
To waste unheard the music of his strains,
And, deaf to all the impertinence of tongue,
That, while it courts, affronts and does you wrong,
Mark well the finish'd plan without a fault,
The seas globose and huge, the o'er-arching vault,
Earth's millions daily fed, a world employ'd
In gathering plenty yet to be enjoy'd,
Till gratitude grew vocal in the praise
Of God, beneficent in all his ways;
Graced with such wisdom, how would beauty shine!

Ye want but that to seem indeed divine.
  Anticipated rents and bills unpaid,
Force many a shining youth into the shade,
Not to redeem his time, but his estate,
And play the fool, but at a cheaper rate.
There, hid in loathed obscurity, removed
From pleasures left, but never more beloved,
He just endures, and with a sickly spleen
Sighs o'er the beauties of the charming scene.
Nature indeed looks prettily, in rhyme;
Streams tinkle sweetly in poetic chime:
The warblings of the blackbird, clear and strong,
Are musical enough in Thomson's song;
And Cobham's groves, and Windsor's green retreats,
When Pope describes them, have a thousand sweets;
He likes the country, but in truth must own,
Most likes it when he studies it in town.
  Poor Jack—no matter who—for when I blame,
I pity, and must therefore sink the name,
Lived in his saddle, loved the chase, the course,
And always, ere he mounted, kiss'd his horse.
The estate, his sires had own'd in ancient years,
Was quickly distanced, match'd against a peer's.
Jack vanish'd, was regretted, and forgot;
'Tis wild good-nature's never failing lot.
At length, when all had long supposed him dead,
By cold submersion, razor, rope, or lead,
My lord, alighting at his usual place,
The Crown, took notice of an ostler's face.
Jack knew his friend, but hoped in that disguise
He might escape the most observing eyes,
And whistling, as if unconcern'd and gay,
Curried his nag and looked another way;
Convinced at last, upon a nearer view,
'Twas he, the same, the very Jack he knew,
O'erwhelm'd at once with wonder, grief, and joy,
He press'd him much to quit his base employ;
His countenance, his purse, his heart, his hand,
Influence and power, were all at his command:
Peers are not always generous as well bred,
But Granby was, meant truly what he said.
Jack bow'd, and was obliged—confess'd 'twas strange,
That so retired he should not wish a change,
But knew no medium between guzzling beer,
And his old stint—three thousand pounds a year.
  Thus some retire to nourish hopeless woe;
Some seeking happiness not found below;
Some to comply with humour, and a mind

To social scenes by nature disinclined;
Some sway'd by fashion, some by deep disgust;
Some self-impoverish'd, and because they must;
But few, that court Retirement, are aware
Of half the toils they must encounter there.
   Lucrative offices are seldom lost
For want of powers proportion'd to the post:
Give e'en a dunce the employment he desires,
And he soon finds the talents it requires;
A business with an income at its heels
Furnishes always oil for its own wheels.
But in his arduous enterprise to close
His active years with indolent repose,
He finds the labours of that state exceed
His utmost faculties, severe indeed.
'Tis easy to resign a toilsome place,
But not to manage leisure with a grace;
Absence of occupation is not rest,
A mind quite vacant is a mind distress'd.
The veteran steed, excused his task at length,
In kind compassion of his failing strength,
And turn'd into the park or mead to graze,
Exempt from future service all his days,
There feels a pleasure perfect in its kind,
Ranges at liberty, and snuffs the wind:
But when his lord would quit the busy road,
To taste a joy like that he has bestow'd,
He proves, less happy than his favour'd brute,
A life of ease a difficult pursuit.
Thought, to the man that never thinks, may seem
As natural as when asleep to dream;
But reveries (for human minds will act)
Specious in show, impossible in fact,
Those flimsy webs, that break as soon as wrought,
Attain not to the dignity of thought:
Nor yet the swarms that occupy the brain,
Where dreams of dress, intrigue, and pleasure reign;
Nor such as useless conversation breeds,
Or lust engenders, and indulgence feeds.
Whence, and what are we? to what end ordain'd?
What means the drama by the world sustain'd?
Business or vain amusement, care or mirth,
Divide the frail inhabitants of earth.
Is duty a mere sport, or an employ?
Life an entrusted talent, or a toy?
Is there, as reason, conscience, Scripture say,
Cause to provide for a great future day,
When, earth's assign'd duration at an end,

Man shall be summon'd and the dead attend?
The trumpet—will it sound? the curtain rise?
And show the august tribunal of the skies,
Where no prevarication shall avail,
Where eloquence and artifice shall fail,
The pride of arrogant distinctions fall,
And conscience and our conduct judge us all?
Pardon me, ye that give the midnight oil
To learned cares or philosophic toil,
Though I revere your honourable names,
Your useful labours, and important aims,
And hold the world indebted to your aid,
Enrich'd with the discoveries ye have made;
Yet let me stand excused, if I esteem
A mind employ'd on so sublime a theme,
Pushing her bold inquiry to the date
And outline of the present transient state,
And, after poising her adventurous wings,
Settling at last upon eternal things,
Far more intelligent, and better taught
The strenuous use of profitable thought,
Than ye, when happiest, and enlighten'd most,
And highest in renown, can justly boast.
    A mind unnerved, or indisposed to bear
The weight of subjects worthiest of her care,
Whatever hopes a change of scene inspires,
Must change her nature, or in vain retires.
An idler is a watch that wants both hands;
As useless if it goes as when it stands.
Books, therefore, not the scandal of the shelves,
In which lewd sensualists print out themselves;
Nor those, in which the stage gives vice a blow,
With what success let modern manners show;
Nor his who, for the bane of thousands born,
Built God a church, and laugh'd his word to scorn,
Skilful alike to seem devout and just,
And stab religion with a sly side-thrust;
Nor those of learn'd philologists, who chase
A panting syllable through time and space
Start it at home, and hunt it in the dark,
To Gaul, to Greece, and into Noah's ark;
But such as learning, without false pretence,
The friend of truth, the associate of sound sense,
And such as, in the zeal of good design,
Strong judgment labouring in the scripture mine,
All such as manly and great souls produce,
Worthy to live, and of eternal use:
Behold in these what leisure hours demand,

Amusement and true knowledge hand in hand.
Luxury gives the mind a childish cast,
And, while she polishes, perverts the taste;
Habits of close attention, thinking heads,
Become more rare as dissipation spreads,
Till authors hear at length one general cry,
Tickle and entertain us, or we die.
The loud demand, from year to year the same,
Beggars invention, and makes fancy lame;
Till farce itself, most mournfully jejune,
Calls for the kind assistance of a tune;
And novels (witness every month's review)
Belie their name, and offer nothing new.
The mind, relaxing into needful sport,
Should turn to writers of an abler sort,
Whose wit well managed, and whose classic style,
Give truth a lustre, and make wisdom smile.
Friends, (for I cannot stint, as some have done,
Too rigid in my view, that name to one;
Though one, I grant it, in the generous breast
Will stand advanced a step above the rest;
Flowers by that name promiscuously we call,
But one, the rose, the regent of them all,)—
Friends, not adopted with a schoolboy's haste,
But chosen with a nice discerning taste,
Well born, well disciplined, who, placed apart
From vulgar minds, have honour much at heart,
And, though the world may think the ingredients odd,
The love of virtue, and the fear of God!
Such friends prevent what else would soon succeed,
A temper rustic as the life we lead,
And keep the polish of the manners clean,
As theirs who bustle in the busiest scene;
For solitude, however some may rave,
Seeming a sanctuary, proves a grave,
A sepulchre, in which the living lie,
Where all good qualities grow sick and die.
I praise the Frenchman, his remark was shrewd,
How sweet, how passing sweet is solitude!
But grant me still a friend in my retreat,
Whom I may whisper—Solitude is sweet.
Yet neither these delights, nor aught beside,
That appetite can ask, or wealth provide,
Can save us always from a tedious day,
Or shine the dulness of still life away;
Divine communion, carefully enjoy'd,
Or sought with energy, must fill the void.
Oh sacred art! to which alone life owes

Its happiest seasons, and a peaceful close,
Scorn'd in a world, indebted to that scorn
For evils daily felt and hardly borne,
Not knowing thee, we reap, with bleeding hands,
Flowers of rank odour upon thorny lands,
And, while experience cautions us in vain,
Grasp seeming happiness, and find it pain.
Despondence, self-deserted in her grief,
Lost by abandoning her own relief,
Murmuring and ungrateful discontent,
That scorns afflictions mercifully meant,
Those humours, tart as wines upon the fret,
Which idleness and weariness beget;
These, and a thousand plagues that haunt the breast,
Fond of the phantom of an earthly rest,
Divine communion chases, as the day
Drives to their dens the obedient beasts of prey.
See Judah's promised king, bereft of all,
Driven out an exile from the face of Saul,
To distant caves the lonely wanderer flies,
To seek that peace a tyrant's frown denies.
Hear the sweet accents of his tuneful voice,
Hear him, o'erwhelm'd with sorrow, yet rejoice;
No womanish or wailing grief has part,
No, not a moment, in his royal heart;
'Tis manly music, such as martyrs make,
Suffering with gladness for a Saviour's sake.
His soul exults, hope animates his lays,
The sense of mercy kindles into praise,
And wilds, familiar with a lion's roar,
Ring with ecstatic sounds unheard before:
'Tis love like his that can alone defeat
The foes of man, or make a desert sweet.
   Religion does not censure or exclude
Unnumber'd pleasures harmlessly pursued;
To study culture, and with artful toil
To meliorate and tame the stubborn soil;
To give dissimilar yet fruitful lands
The grain, or herb, or plant that each demands;
To cherish virtue in an humble state,
And share the joys your bounty may create;
To mark the matchless workings of the power
That shuts within its seed the future flower,
Bids these in elegance of form excel,
In colour these, and those delight the smell,
Sends Nature forth the daughter of the skies,
To dance on earth, and charm all human eyes;
To teach the canvas innocent deceit,

Or lay the landscape on the snowy sheet—
These, these are arts pursued without a crime,
That leave no stain upon the wing of time.
   Me poetry (or, rather, notes that aim
Feebly and vainly at poetic fame)
Employs, shut out from more important views,
Fast by the banks of the slow-winding Ouse;
Content if, thus sequester'd, I may raise
A monitor's, though not a poet's, praise,
And, while I teach an art too little known,
To close life wisely, may not waste my own.

AN EPISTLE TO JOSEPH HILL, ESQ.

Dear Joseph—five-and-twenty years ago—
Alas, how time escapes!—'tis even so—
With frequent intercourse, and always sweet,
And always friendly, we were wont to cheat
A tedious hour—and now we never meet!
As some grave gentleman in Terence says,
('Twas therefore much the same in ancient days,)
Good lack, we know not what to-morrow brings—
Strange fluctuation of all human things!
True. Changes will befall, and friends may part,
But distance only cannot change the heart:
And, were I call'd to prove the assertion true,
One proof should serve—a reference to you.
   Whence comes it then, that, in the wane of life,
Though nothing have occurr'd to kindle strife,
We find the friends we fancied we had won,
Though numerous once, reduced to few or none?
Can gold grow worthless that has stood the touch?
No; gold they seem'd, but they were never such.
   Horatio's servant once, with bow and cringe,
Swinging the parlour door upon its hinge,
Dreading a negative, and overawed
Lest he should trespass, begg'd to go abroad.
Go, fellow!—whither?—turning short about—
Nay—stay at home—you're always going out.
'Tis but a step, sir, just at the street's end.—
For what?—An please you, sir, to see a friend.—
A friend! Horatio cried, and seem'd to start—
Yea marry shalt thou, and with all my heart.
And fetch my cloak; for though the night be raw,
I'll see him too—the first I ever saw.
   I knew the man, and knew his nature mild,

And was his plaything often when a child;
But somewhat at that moment pinch'd him close,
Else he was seldom bitter or morose.
Perhaps, his confidence just then betray'd,
His grief might prompt him with the speech he made;
Perhaps 'twas mere good humour gave it birth,
The harmless play of pleasantry and mirth.
Howe'er it was, his language, in my mind,
Bespoke at least a man that knew mankind.
　But not to moralize too much, and strain
To prove an evil of which all complain;
(I hate long arguments verbosely spun;)
One story more, dear Hill, and I have done.
Once on a time an emperor, a wise man,
No matter where, in China or Japan,
Decreed that whosoever should offend
Against the well-known duties of a friend,
Convicted once, should ever after wear
But half a coat, and show his bosom bare.
The punishment importing this, no doubt,
That all was naught within, and all found out.
　Oh, happy Britain! we have not to fear
Such hard and arbitrary measure here;
Else, could a law like that which I relate
Once have the sanction of our triple state,
Some few, that I have known in days of old,
Would run most dreadful risk of catching cold;
While you, my friend, whatever wind should blow,
Might traverse England safely to and fro,
An honest man, close-button'd to the chin,
Broad-cloth without, and a warm heart within.

TIROCINIUM; OR, A REVIEW OF SCHOOLS

Κεφαλαιον δη παιδειας ορθη τροφη. —Plato
Αρχη κολιτειας απασης τροφα. —Diog. Laert.

To the Rev. William Cawthorne Unwin, Rector of Stock in Essex, the tutor of his two sons, the following poem, recommending private tuition in preference to an education at school, is inscribed, by his affectionate friend,

William Cowper.
Olney, Nov. 6, 1784.

It is not from his form, in which we trace
Strength join'd with beauty, dignity with grace,

That man, the master of this globe, derives
His right of empire over all that lives.
That form, indeed, the associate of a mind
Vast in its powers, ethereal in its kind,
That form, the labour of Almighty skill,
Framed for the service of a freeborn will,
Asserts precedence, and bespeaks control,
But borrows all its grandeur from the soul.
Hers is the state, the splendour, and the throne,
An intellectual kingdom, all her own.
For her the memory fills her ample page
With truths pour'd down from every distant age;
For her amasses an unbounded store,
The wisdom of great nations, now no more;
Though laden, not encumber'd with her spoil;
Laborious, yet unconscious of her toil;
When copiously supplied, then most enlarged;
Still to be fed, and not to be surcharged.
For her the Fancy, roving unconfined,
The present muse of every pensive mind,
Works magic wonders, adds a brighter hue
To Nature's scenes than Nature ever knew.
At her command winds rise and waters roar,
Again she lays them slumbering on the shore;
With flower and fruit the wilderness supplies,
Or bids the rocks in ruder pomp arise.
For her the Judgment, umpire in the strife
That Grace and Nature have to wage through life,
Quick-sighted arbiter of good and ill,
Appointed sage preceptor to the Will,
Condemns, approves, and with a faithful voice
Guides the decision of a doubtful choice.

Why did the fiat of a God give birth
To yon fair Sun and his attendant Earth?
And, when descending he resigns the skies,
Why takes the gentler Moon her turn to rise,
Whom Ocean feels through all his countless waves,
And owns her power on every shore he laves?
Why do the seasons still enrich the year,
Fruitful and young as in their first career?
Spring hangs her infant blossoms on the trees,
Rock'd in the cradle of the western breeze;
Summer in haste the thriving charge receives
Beneath the shade of her expanded leaves,
Till Autumn's fiercer heats and plenteous dews
Dye them at last in all their glowing hues.—
'Twere wild profusion all, and bootless waste,

Power misemploy'd, munificence misplaced,
Had not its Author dignified the plan,
And crown'd it with the majesty of man.
Thus form'd, thus placed, intelligent, and taught,
Look where he will, the wonders God has wrought,
The wildest scorner of his Maker's laws
Finds in a sober moment time to pause,
To press the important question on his heart,
"Why form'd at all, and wherefore as thou art?"
If man be what he seems, this hour a slave,
The next mere dust and ashes in the grave;
Endued with reason only to descry
His crimes and follies with an aching eye;
With passions, just that he may prove, with pain,
The force he spends against their fury vain;
And if, soon after having burnt, by turns,
With every lust with which frail Nature burns,
His being end where death dissolves the bond,
The tomb take all, and all be blank beyond;
Then he, of all that Nature has brought forth,
Stands self-impeach'd the creature of least worth,
And, useless while he lives, and when he dies,
Brings into doubt the wisdom of the skies.

Truths that the learn'd pursue with eager thought
Are not important always as dear-bought,
Proving at last, though told in pompous strains,
A childish waste of philosophic pains;
But truths on which depends our main concern,
That 'tis our shame and misery not to learn,
Shine by the side of every path we tread
With such a lustre, he that runs may read.
'Tis true that, if to trifle life away
Down to the sunset of their latest day,
Then perish on futurity's wide shore
Like fleeting exhalations, found no more,
Were all that heaven required of human kind,
And all the plan their destiny design'd,
What none could reverence all might justly blame,
And man would breathe but for his Maker's shame.
But reason heard, and nature well perused,
At once the dreaming mind is disabused.
If all we find possessing earth, sea, air,
Reflect His attributes who placed them there,
Fulfil the purpose, and appear design'd
Proofs of the wisdom of the all-seeing mind,
'Tis plain the creature, whom he chose to invest
With kingship and dominion o'er the rest,

Received his nobler nature, and was made
Fit for the power in which he stands arrayed;
That first, or last, hereafter, if not here,
He too might make his author's wisdom clear,
Praise him on earth, or, obstinately dumb,
Suffer his justice in a world to come.
This once believed, 'twere logic misapplied
To prove a consequence by none denied,
That we are bound to cast the minds of youth
Betimes into the mould of heavenly truth,
That taught of God they may indeed be wise,
Nor ignorantly wandering miss the skies.

In early days the conscience has in most
A quickness, which in later life is lost:
Preserved from guilt by salutary fears,
Or guilty soon relenting into tears.
Too careless often, as our years proceed,
What friends we sort with, or what books we read,
Our parents yet exert a prudent care
To feed our infant minds with proper fare;
And wisely store the nursery by degrees
With wholesome learning, yet acquired with ease.
Neatly secured from being soil'd or torn
Beneath a pane of thin translucent horn,
A book (to please us at a tender age
'Tis call'd a book, though but a single page)
Presents the prayer the Saviour deign'd to teach,
Which children use, and parsons—when they preach.
Lisping our syllables, we scramble next
Through moral narrative, or sacred text;
And learn with wonder how this world began,
Who made, who marr'd, and who has ransom'd man:
Points which, unless the Scripture made them plain,
The wisest heads might agitate in vain.
Oh thou, whom, borne on fancy's eager wing
Back to the season of life's happy spring,
I pleased remember, and, while memory yet
Holds fast her office here, can ne'er forget;
Ingenious dreamer, in whose well-told tale
Sweet fiction and sweet truth alike prevail;
Whose humorous vein, strong sense, and simple style,
May teach the gayest, make the gravest smile;
Witty, and well employ'd, and, like thy Lord,
Speaking in parables his slighted word;
I name thee not, lest so despised a name
Should move a sneer at thy deserved fame;
Yet e'en in transitory life's late day,

That mingles all my brown with sober grey,
Revere the man whose Pilgrim marks the road,
And guides the Progress of the soul to God.
'Twere well with most, if books that could engage
Their childhood pleased them at a riper age;
The man, approving what had charm'd the boy,
Would die at last in comfort, peace, and joy,
And not with curses on his heart, who stole
The gem of truth from his unguarded soul.
The stamp of artless piety impress'd
By kind tuition on his yielding breast,
The youth, now bearded and yet pert and raw,
Regards with scorn, though once received with awe;
And, warp'd into the labyrinth of lies,
That babblers, call'd philosophers, devise,
Blasphemes his creed, as founded on a plan
Replete with dreams, unworthy of a man.
Touch but his nature in its ailing part,
Assert the native evil of his heart,
His pride resents the charge, although the proof
Rise in his forehead, and seem rank enough:
Point to the cure, describe a Saviour's cross
As God's expedient to retrieve his loss,
The young apostate sickens at the view,
And hates it with the malice of a Jew.

How weak the barrier of mere nature proves,
Opposed against the pleasures nature loves!
While self-betray'd, and wilfully undone,
She longs to yield, no sooner wooed than won.
Try now the merits of this blest exchange
Of modest truth for wit's eccentric range.
Time was, he closed as he began the day,
With decent duty, not ashamed to pray;
The practice was a bond upon his heart,
A pledge he gave for a consistent part;
Nor could he dare presumptuously displease
A power confess'd so lately on his knees.
But now farewell all legendary tales,
The shadows fly, philosophy prevails;
Prayer to the winds, and caution to the waves;
Religion makes the free by nature slaves.
Priests have invented, and the world admired
What knavish priests promulgate as inspired;
Till Reason, now no longer overawed,
Resumes her powers, and spurns the clumsy fraud;
And, common sense diffusing real day,
The meteor of the Gospel dies away.

Such rhapsodies our shrewd discerning youth
Learn from expert inquirers after truth;
Whose only care, might truth presume to speak,
Is not to find what they profess to seek.
And thus, well tutor'd only while we share
A mother's lectures and a nurse's care;
And taught at schools much mythologic stuff,
But sound religion sparingly enough;
Our early notices of truth disgraced,
Soon lose their credit, and are all effaced.
Would you your son should be a sot or dunce,
Lascivious, headstrong, or all these at once;
That in good time the stripling's finish'd taste
For loose expense and fashionable waste
Should prove your ruin, and his own at last;
Train him in public with a mob of boys,
Childish in mischief only and in noise,
Else of a mannish growth, and five in ten
In infidelity and lewdness men.
There shall he learn, ere sixteen winters old,
That authors are most useful pawn'd or sold;
That pedantry is all that schools impart,
But taverns teach the knowledge of the heart;
There waiter Dick, with bacchanalian lays,
Shall win his heart, and have his drunken praise,
His counsellor and bosom friend shall prove,
And some street-pacing harlot his first love.
Schools, unless discipline were doubly strong,
Detain their adolescent charge too long;
The management of tiros of eighteen
Is difficult, their punishment obscene.
The stout tall captain, whose superior size
The minor heroes view with envious eyes,
Becomes their pattern, upon whom they fix
Their whole attention, and ape all his tricks.
His pride, that scorns to obey or to submit,
With them is courage; his effrontery wit.
His wild excursions, window-breaking feats,
Robbery of gardens, quarrels in the streets,
His hairbreadth 'scapes, and all his daring schemes,
Transport them, and are made their favourite themes.
In little bosoms such achievements strike
A kindred spark: they burn to do the like.
Thus, half accomplish'd ere he yet begin
To show the peeping down upon his chin;
And, as maturity of years comes on,
Made just the adept that you design'd your son;
To ensure the perseverance of his course,

And give your monstrous project all its force,
Send him to college. If he there be tamed,
Or in one article of vice reclaim'd,
Where no regard of ordinances is shown
Or look'd for now, the fault must be his own.
Some sneaking virtue, lurks in him, no doubt,
Where neither strumpets' charms, nor drinking bout,
Nor gambling practices can find it out.
Such youths of spirit, and that spirit too,
Ye nurseries of our boys, we owe to you:
Though from ourselves the mischief more proceeds,
For public schools 'tis public folly feeds.
The slaves of custom and establish'd mode,
With packhorse constancy we keep the road,
Crooked or straight, through quags or thorny dells,
True to the jingling of our leader's bells.
To follow foolish precedents, and wink
With both our eyes, is easier than to think:
And such an age as ours balks no expense,
Except of caution and of common sense;
Else sure notorious fact, and proof so plain,
Would turn our steps into a wiser train.
I blame not those who, with what care they can,
O'erwatch the numerous and unruly clan;
Or, if I blame, 'tis only that they dare
Promise a work of which they must despair.
Have ye, ye sage intendants of the whole,
A ubiquarian presence and control,
Elisha's eye, that, when Gehazi stray'd,
Went with him, and saw all the game he play'd?
Yes—ye are conscious; and on all the shelves
Your pupils strike upon have struck yourselves.
Or if, by nature sober, ye had then,
Boys as ye were, the gravity of men,
Ye knew at least, by constant proofs address'd
To ears and eyes, the vices of the rest.
But ye connive at what ye cannot cure,
And evils not to be endured endure,
Lest power exerted, but without success,
Should make the little ye retain still less.
Ye once were justly famed for bringing forth
Undoubted scholarship and genuine worth;
And in the firmament of fame still shines
A glory, bright as that of all the signs,
Of poets raised by you, and statesmen, and divines.
Peace to them all! those brilliant times are fled,
And no such lights are kindling in their stead.
Our striplings shine indeed, but with such rays

As set the midnight riot in a blaze;
And seem, if judged by their expressive looks,
Deeper in none than in their surgeons' books.
  Say, muse, (for education made the song,
No muse can hesitate, or linger long,)
What causes move us, knowing, as we must,
That these ménageries all fail their trust,
To send our sons to scout and scamper there,
While colts and puppies cost us so much care?
  Be it a weakness, it deserves some praise,
We love the play-place of our early days;
The scene is touching, and the heart is stone
That feels not at that sight, and feels at none.
The wall on which we tried our graving skill,
The very name we carved subsisting still;
The bench on which we sat while deep employ'd,
Though mangled, hack'd, and hew'd, not yet destroy'd;
The little ones, unbutton'd, glowing hot,
Playing our games, and on the very spot;
As happy as we once, to kneel and draw
The chalky ring, and knuckle down at taw;
To pitch the ball into the grounded hat,
Or drive it devious with a dextrous pat;
The pleasing spectacle at once excites
Such recollection of our own delights,
That, viewing it, we seem almost to obtain
Our innocent sweet simple years again.
This fond attachment to the well-known place,
Whence first we started into life's long race,
Maintains its hold with such unfailing sway,
We feel it e'en in age, and at our latest day.
Hark! how the sire of chits, whose future share
Of classic food begins to be his care,
With his own likeness placed on either knee,
Indulges all a father's heartfelt glee;
And tells them, as he strokes their silver locks,
That they must soon learn Latin, and to box;
Then turning, he regales his listening wife
With all the adventures of his early life;
His skill in coachmanship, or driving chaise,
In bilking tavern-bills, and spouting plays;
What shifts he used, detected in a scrape,
How he was flogg'd, or had the luck to escape;
What sums he lost at play, and how he sold
Watch, seals, and all—till all his pranks are told.
Retracing thus his frolics, ('tis a name
That palliates deeds of folly and of shame,)
He gives the local bias all its sway;

Resolves that where he play'd his sons shall play,
And destines their bright genius to be shown
Just in the scene where he display'd his own.
The meek and bashful boy will soon be taught
To be as bold and forward as he ought;
The rude will scuffle through with ease enough,
Great schools suit best the sturdy and the rough.
Ah, happy designation, prudent choice,
The event is sure; expect it, and rejoice!
Soon see your wish fulfill'd in either child,
The pert made perter, and the tame made wild.
   The great indeed, by titles, riches, birth,
Excused the incumbrance of more solid worth,
Are best disposed of where with most success
They may acquire that confident address,
Those habits of profuse and lewd expense,
That scorn of all delights but those of sense,
Which, though in plain plebeians we condemn,
With so much reason, all expect from them.
But families of less illustrious fame,
Whose chief distinction is their spotless name,
Whose heirs, their honours none, their income small,
Must shine by true desert, or not at all,
What dream they of, that, with so little care
They risk their hopes, their dearest treasure, there?
They dream of little Charles or William graced
With wig prolix, down flowing to his waist;
They see the attentive crowds his talents draw,
They hear him speak—the oracle of law.
The father, who designs his babe a priest,
Dreams him episcopally such at least;
And, while the playful jockey scours the room
Briskly, astride upon the parlour broom,
In fancy sees him more superbly ride
In coach with purple lined, and mitres on its side.
Events improbable and strange as these,
Which only a parental eye foresees,
A public school shall bring to pass with ease.
But how? resides such virtue in that air,
As must create an appetite for prayer?
And will it breathe into him all the zeal
That candidates for such a prize should feel,
To take the lead and be the foremost still
In all true worth and literary skill?
"Ah, blind to bright futurity, untaught
The knowledge of the World, and dull of thought!
Church-ladders are not always mounted best
By learned clerks and Latinists profess'd.

The exalted prize demands an upward look,
Not to be found by poring on a book.
Small skill in Latin, and still less in Greek,
Is more than adequate to all I seek.
Let erudition grace him, or not grace,
I give the bauble but the second place;
His wealth, fame, honours, all that I intend,
Subsist and centre in one point—a friend.
A friend, whate'er he studies or neglects,
Shall give him consequence, heal all defects.
His intercourse with peers and sons of peers—
There dawns the splendour of his future years:
In that bright quarter his propitious skies
Shall blush betimes, and there his glory rise.
Your Lordship, and Your Grace! what school can teach
A rhetoric equal to those parts of speech?
What need of Homer's verse or Tully's prose,
Sweet interjections! if he learn but those?
Let reverend churls his ignorance rebuke,
Who starve upon a dog's ear'd Pentateuch,
The parson knows enough who knows a duke."
Egregious purpose! worthily begun
In barbarous prostitution of your son;
Press'd on his part by means that would disgrace
A scrivener's clerk, or footman out of place,
And ending, if at last its end be gain'd,
In sacrilege, in God's own house profaned.
It may succeed; and, if his sins should call
For more than common punishment, it shall;
The wretch shall rise, and be the thing on earth
Least qualified in honour, learning, worth,
To occupy a sacred, awful post,
In which the best and worthiest tremble most.
The royal letters are a thing of course,
A king, that would, might recommend his horse;
And deans, no doubt, and chapters, with one voice,
As bound in duty, would confirm the choice.
Behold your bishop! well he plays his part,
Christian in name, and infidel in heart,
Ghostly in office, earthly in his plan,
A slave at court, elsewhere a lady's man.
Dumb as a senator, and as a priest
A piece of mere church furniture at best;
To live estranged from God his total scope,
And his end sure, without one glimpse of hope.
But, fair although and feasible it seem,
Depend not much upon your golden dream;
For Providence, that seems concern'd to exempt

The hallow'd bench from absolute contempt,
In spite of all the wrigglers into place,
Still keeps a seat or two for worth and grace;
And therefore 'tis, that, though the sight be rare,
We sometimes see a Lowth or Bagot there.
Besides, school friendships are not always found,
Though fair in promise, permanent and sound;
The most disinterested and virtuous minds,
In early years connected, time unbinds
New situations give a different cast
Of habit, inclination, temper, taste;
And he, that seem'd our counterpart at first,
Soon shows the strong similitude reversed.
Young heads are giddy, and young hearts are warm,
And make mistakes for manhood to reform.
Boys are, at best, but pretty buds unblown,
Whose scent and hues are rather guess'd than known;
Each dreams that each is just what he appears,
But learns his error in maturer years,
When disposition, like a sail unfurl'd,
Shows all its rents and patches to the world.
If, therefore, e'en when honest in design,
A boyish friendship may so soon decline,
'Twere wiser sure to inspire a little heart
With just abhorrence of so mean a part,
Than set your son to work at a vile trade
For wages so unlikely to be paid.
   Our public hives of puerile resort,
That are of chief and most approved report,
To such base hopes, in many a sordid soul,
Owe their repute in part, but not the whole.
A principle, whose proud pretensions pass
Unquestion'd, though the jewel be but glass—
That with a world, not often over-nice,
Ranks as a virtue, and is yet a vice;
Or rather a gross compound, justly tried,
Of envy, hatred, jealousy, and pride—
Contributes most, perhaps, to enhance their fame;
And emulation is its specious name.
Boys, once on fire with that contentious zeal,
Feel all the rage that female rivals feel;
The prize of beauty in a woman's eyes
Not brighter than in theirs the scholar's prize.
The spirit of that competition burns
With all varieties of ill by turns;
Each vainly magnifies his own success,
Resents his fellow's, wishes it were less,
Exults in his miscarriage if he fail,

Deems his reward too great if he prevail,
And labours to surpass him day and night,
Less for improvement than to tickle spite.
The spur is powerful, and I grant its force;
It pricks the genius forward in its course,
Allows short time for play, and none for sloth;
And, felt alike by each, advances both:
But judge, where so much evil intervenes,
The end, though plausible, not worth the means.
Weigh, for a moment, classical desert
Against a heart depraved and temper hurt;
Hurt too perhaps for life; for early wrong
Done to the nobler part affects it long;
And you are staunch indeed in learning's cause,
If you can crown a discipline, that draws
Such mischiefs after it, with much applause.
    Connexion form'd for interest, and endear'd
By selfish views, thus censured and cashier'd;
And emulation, as engendering hate,
Doom'd to a no less ignominious fate:
The props of such proud seminaries fall,
The Jachin and the Boaz of them all.
Great schools rejected then, as those that swell
Beyond a size that can be managed well,
Shall royal institutions miss the bays,
And small academies win all the praise?
Force not my drift beyond its just intent,
I praise a school as Pope a government;
So take my judgment in his language dress'd,
"Whate'er is best administer'd is best."
Few boys are born with talents that excel,
But all are capable of living well;
Then ask not, whether limited or large?
But, watch they strictly, or neglect their charge?
If anxious only that their boys may learn,
While morals languish, a despised concern,
The great and small deserve one common blame,
Different in size, but in effect the same.
Much zeal in virtue's cause all teachers boast,
Though motives of mere lucre sway the most;
Therefore in towns and cities they abound,
For there the game they seek is easiest found;
Though there, in spite of all that care can do,
Traps to catch youth are most abundant too.
If shrewd, and of a well-constructed brain,
Keen in pursuit, and vigorous to retain,
Your son come forth a prodigy of skill;
As, wheresoever taught, so form'd, he will;

The pedagogue, with self-complacent air,
Claims more than half the praise as his due share.
But if, with all his genius, he betray,
Not more intelligent than loose and gay,
Such vicious habits as disgrace his name,
Threaten his health, his fortune, and his fame;
Though want of due restraint alone have bred
The symptoms that you see with so much dread;
Unenvied there, he may sustain alone
The whole reproach, the fault was all his own.
   Oh! 'tis a sight to be with joy perused,
By all whom sentiment has not abused;
New-fangled sentiment, the boasted grace
Of those who never feel in the right place;
A sight surpass'd by none that we can show,
Though Vestris on one leg still shine below;
A father blest with an ingenuous son,
Father, and friend, and tutor, all in one.
How!—turn again to tales long since forgot,
Æsop, and Phædrus, and the rest?—Why not?
He will not blush, that has a father's heart,
To take in childish plays a childish part;
But bends his sturdy back to any toy
That youth takes pleasure in, to please his boy:
Then why resign into a stranger's hand
A task as much within your own command,
That God and nature, and your interest too,
Seem with one voice to delegate to you?
Why hire a lodging in a house unknown
For one whose tenderest thoughts all hover round your own?
This second weaning, needless as it is,
How does it lacerate both your heart and his!
The indented stick, that loses day by day,
Notch after notch, till all are smooth'd away,
Bears witness, long ere his dismission come,
With what intense desire he wants his home.
But though the joys he hopes beneath your roof
Bid fair enough to answer in the proof,
Harmless, and safe, and natural, as they are,
A disappointment waits him even there:
Arrived, he feels an unexpected change;
He blushes, hangs his head, is shy and strange,
No longer takes, as once, with fearless ease,
His favourite stand between his father's knees,
But seeks the corner of some distant seat,
And eyes the door, and watches a retreat,
And, least familiar where he should be most,
Feels all his happiest privileges lost.

Alas, poor boy!—the natural effect
Of love by absence chill'd into respect.
Say, what accomplishments, at school acquired,
Brings he, to sweeten fruits so undesired?
Thou well deserv'st an alienated son,
Unless thy conscious heart acknowledge—none;
None that, in thy domestic snug recess,
He had not made his own with more address,
Though some, perhaps, that shock thy feeling mind,
And better never learn'd, or left behind.
Add too, that, thus estranged, thou canst obtain
By no kind arts his confidence again;
That here begins with most that long complaint
Of filial frankness lost, and love grown faint,
Which, oft neglected, in life's waning years
A parent pours into regardless ears.
  Like caterpillars, dangling under trees
By slender threads, and swinging in the breeze,
Which filthily bewray and sore disgrace
The boughs in which are bred the unseemly race;
While every worm industriously weaves
And winds his web about the rivell'd leaves;
So numerous are the follies that annoy
The mind and heart of every sprightly boy;
Imaginations noxious and perverse,
Which admonition can alone disperse.
The encroaching nuisance asks a faithful hand,
Patient, affectionate, of high command,
To check the procreation of a breed
Sure to exhaust the plant on which they feed.
'Tis not enough that Greek or Roman page,
At stated hours, his freakish thoughts engage;
E'en in his pastimes he requires a friend
To warn, and teach him safely to unbend;
O'er all his pleasures gently to preside,
Watch his emotions, and control their tide;
And levying thus, and with an easy sway,
A tax of profit from his very play,
To impress a value, not to be erased,
On moments squander'd else, and running all to waste.
And seems it nothing in a father's eye
That unimproved those many moments fly?
And is he well content his son should find
No nourishment to feed his growing mind,
But conjugated verbs and nouns declined?
For such is all the mental food purveyed
By public hackneys in the schooling trade;
Who feed a pupil's intellect with store

Of syntax, truly, but with little more;
Dismiss their cares when they dismiss their flock,
Machines themselves, and govern'd by a clock.
Perhaps a father, blest with any brains,
Would deem it no abuse, or waste of pains,
To improve this diet, at no great expense,
With savoury truth and wholesome common sense;
To lead his son, for prospects of delight,
To some not steep, though philosophic, height,
Thence to exhibit to his wondering eyes
Yon circling worlds, their distance, and their size,
The moons of Jove, and Saturn's belted ball,
And the harmonious order of them all;
To show him in an insect or a flower
Such microscopic proof of skill and power,
As, hid from ages past, God now displays
To combat atheists with in modern days;
To spread the earth before him, and commend,
With designation of the finger's end,
Its various parts to his attentive note,
Thus bringing home to him the most remote;
To teach his heart to glow with generous flame,
Caught from the deeds of men of ancient fame;
And, more than all, with commendation due,
To set some living worthy in his view,
Whose fair example may at once inspire
A wish to copy what he must admire.
Such knowledge, gain'd betimes, and which appears,
Though solid, not too weighty for his years,
Sweet in itself, and not forbidding sport,
When health demands it, of athletic sort,
Would make him—what some lovely boys have been,
And more than one perhaps that I have seen—
An evidence and reprehension both
Of the mere schoolboy's lean and tardy growth.
  Art thou a man professionally tied,
With all thy faculties elsewhere applied,
Too busy to intend a meaner care
Than how to enrich thyself, and next thine heir;
Or art thou (as, though rich, perhaps thou art)
But poor in knowledge, having none to impart:—
Behold that figure, neat, though plainly clad;
His sprightly mingled with a shade of sad;
Not of a nimble tongue, though now and then
Heard to articulate like other men;
No jester, and yet lively in discourse,
His phrase well chosen, clear, and full of force;
And his address, if not quite French in ease,

Not English stiff, but frank, and form'd to please;
Low in the world, because he scorns its arts;
A man of letters, manners, morals, parts;
Unpatronized, and therefore little known;
Wise for himself and his few friends alone—
In him thy well-appointed proxy see,
Arm'd for a work too difficult for thee;
Prepared by taste, by learning, and true worth,
To form thy son, to strike his genius forth;
Beneath thy roof, beneath thine eye, to prove
The force of discipline when back'd by love;
To double all thy pleasure in thy child,
His mind inform'd, his morals undefiled.
Safe under such a wing, the boy shall show
No spots contracted among grooms below,
Nor taint his speech with meannesses, design'd
By footman Tom for witty and refined.
There, in his commerce with the liveried herd,
Lurks the contagion chiefly to be fear'd;
For since (so fashion dictates) all, who claim
A higher than a mere plebeian fame,
Find it expedient, come what mischief may,
To entertain a thief or two in pay,
(And they that can afford the expense of more,
Some half a dozen, and some half a score,)
Great cause occurs to save him from a band
So sure to spoil him, and so near at hand;
A point secured, if once he be supplied
With some such Mentor always at his side.
Are such men rare? perhaps they would abound
Were occupation easier to be found,
Were education, else so sure to fail,
Conducted on a manageable scale,
And schools, that have outlived all just esteem,
Exchanged for the secure domestic scheme.—
But, having found him, be thou duke or earl,
Show thou hast sense enough to prize the pearl,
And, as thou wouldst the advancement of thine heir
In all good faculties beneath his care,
Respect, as is but rational and just,
A man deem'd worthy of so dear a trust.
Despised by thee, what more can he expect
From youthful folly than the same neglect?
A flat and fatal negative obtains
That instant upon all his future pains;
His lessons tire, his mild rebukes offend,
And all the instructions of thy son's best friend
Are a stream choked, or trickling to no end.

Doom him not then to solitary meals;
But recollect that he has sense, and feels;
And that, possessor of a soul refined,
An upright heart, and cultivated mind,
His post not mean, his talents not unknown,
He deems it hard to vegetate alone.
And, if admitted at thy board he sit,
Account him no just mark for idle wit;
Offend not him, whom modesty restrains
From repartee, with jokes that he disdains;
Much less transfix his feelings with an oath;
Nor frown, unless he vanish with the cloth.—
And, trust me, his utility may reach
To more than he is hired or bound to teach;
Much trash unutter'd, and some ills undone,
Through reverence of the censor of thy son.
   But, if thy table be indeed unclean,
Foul with excess, and with discourse obscene,
And thou a wretch, whom, following her old plan,
The world accounts an honourable man,
Because forsooth thy courage has been tried,
And stood the test, perhaps on the wrong side;
Though thou hadst never grace enough to prove
That any thing but vice could win thy love;—
Or hast thou a polite, card-playing wife,
Chain'd to the routs that she frequents for life;
Who, just when industry begins to snore,
Flies, wing'd with joy, to some coach-crowded door;
And thrice in every winter throngs thine own
With half the chariots and sedans in town
Thyself meanwhile e'en shifting as thou mayst;
Not very sober though, nor very chaste;
Or is thine house, though less superb thy rank,
If not a scene of pleasure, a mere blank,
And thou at best, and in thy soberest mood,
A trifler vain, and empty of all good;—
Though mercy for thyself thou canst have none,
Hear Nature plead, show mercy to thy son.
Saved from his home, where every day brings forth
Some mischief fatal to his future worth,
Find him a better in a distant spot,
Within some pious pastor's humble cot,
Where vile example (yours I chiefly mean,
The most seducing, and the oftenest seen)
May never more be stamp'd upon his breast,
Not yet perhaps incurably impress'd.
Where early rest makes early rising sure,
Disease or comes not, or finds easy cure,

Prevented much by diet neat and plain;
Or, if it enter, soon starved out again:
Where all the attention of his faithful host,
Discreetly limited to two at most,
May raise such fruits as shall reward his care,
And not at last evaporate in air:
Where, stillness aiding study, and his mind
Serene, and to his duties much inclined,
Not occupied in day dreams, as at home,
Of pleasures past, or follies yet to come,
His virtuous toil may terminate at last
In settled habit and decided taste.—
But whom do I advise? the fashion-led,
The incorrigibly wrong, the deaf, the dead!
Whom care and cool deliberation suit
Not better much than spectacles a brute;
Who, if their sons some slight tuition share,
Deem it of no great moment whose, or where;
Too proud to adopt the thoughts of one unknown,
And much too gay to have any of their own.
But courage, man! methought the Muse replied,
Mankind are various, and the world is wide:
The ostrich, silliest of the feather'd kind,
And form'd of God without a parent's mind,
Commits her eggs, incautious, to the dust,
Forgetful that the foot may crush the trust;
And, while on public nurseries they rely,
Not knowing, and too oft not caring, why,
Irrational in what they thus prefer,
No few, that would seem wise, resemble her.
But all are not alike. Thy warning voice
May here and there prevent erroneous choice;
And some, perhaps, who, busy as they are,
Yet make their progeny their dearest care,
(Whose hearts will ache, once told what ills may reach
Their offspring, left upon so wild a beach,)
Will need no stress of argument to enforce
The expedience of a less adventurous course:
The rest will slight thy counsel, or condemn;
But they have human feelings—turn to them.
  To you, then, tenants of life's middle state,
Securely placed between the small and great,
Whose character, yet undebauch'd, retains
Two-thirds of all the virtue that remains,
Who, wise yourselves, desire your sons should learn
Your wisdom and your ways—to you I turn.
Look round you on a world perversely blind;
See what contempt is fallen on human kind;

See wealth abused, and dignities misplaced,
Great titles, offices, and trusts disgraced,
Long lines of ancestry, renown'd of old,
Their noble qualities all quench'd and cold;
See Bedlam's closeted and handcuff'd charge
Surpass'd in frenzy by the mad at large;
See great commanders making war a trade,
Great lawyers, lawyers without study made;
Churchmen, in whose esteem their best employ
Is odious, and their wages all their joy,
Who, far enough from furnishing their shelves
With Gospel lore, turn infidels themselves;
See womanhood despised, and manhood shamed
With infamy too nauseous to be named,
Fops at all corners, ladylike in mien,
Civited fellows, smelt ere they are seen,
Else coarse and rude in manners, and their tongue
On fire with curses, and with nonsense hung,
Now flush'd with drunkenness, now with whoredom pale,
Their breath a sample of last night's regale;
See volunteers in all the vilest arts,
Men well endow'd, of honourable parts,
Design'd by Nature wise, but self-made fools;
All these, and more like these, were bred at schools.
And if it chance, as sometimes chance it will,
That though school-bred the boy be virtuous still;
Such rare exceptions, shining in the dark,
Prove, rather than impeach, the just remark:
As here and there a twinkling star descried
Serves but to show how black is all beside.
Now look on him, whose very voice in tone
Just echoes thine, whose features are thine own,
And stroke his polish'd cheek of purest red,
And lay thine hand upon his flaxen head,
And say, My boy, the unwelcome hour is come,
When thou, transplanted from thy genial home,
Must find a colder soil and bleaker air,
And trust for safety to a stranger's care;
What character, what turn thou wilt assume
From constant converse with I know not whom;
Who there will court thy friendship, with what views,
And, artless as thou art, whom thou wilt choose;
Though much depends on what thy choice shall be,
Is all chance-medley, and unknown to me.
Canst thou, the tear just trembling on thy lids,
And while the dreadful risk foreseen forbids;
Free too, and under no constraining force,
Unless the sway of custom warp thy course;

Lay such a stake upon the losing side,
Merely to gratify so blind a guide?
Thou canst not! Nature, pulling at thine heart,
Condemns the unfatherly, the imprudent part.
Thou wouldst not, deaf to Nature's tenderest plea,
Turn him adrift upon a rolling sea,
Nor say, Go thither, conscious that there lay
A brood of asps, or quicksands in his way;
Then, only govern'd by the self-same rule
Of natural pity, send him not to school.
No—guard him better. Is he not thine own,
Thyself in miniature, thy flesh, thy bone?
And hopest thou not, ('tis every father's hope,)
That, since thy strength must with thy years elope,
And thou wilt need some comfort to assuage
Health's last farewell, a staff of thine old age,
That then, in recompence of all thy cares,
Thy child shall show respect to thy grey hairs,
Befriend thee, of all other friends bereft,
And give thy life its only cordial left?
Aware then how much danger intervenes,
To compass that good end, forecast the means.
His heart, now passive, yields to thy command;
Secure it thine, its key is in thine hand;
If thou desert thy charge, and throw it wide,
Nor heed what guests there enter and abide,
Complain not if attachments lewd and base
Supplant thee in it and usurp thy place.
But, if thou guard its sacred chambers sure
From vicious inmates and delights impure,
Either his gratitude shall hold him fast,
And keep him warm and filial to the last;
Or, if he prove unkind, (as who can say
But, being man, and therefore frail, he may?)
One comfort yet shall cheer thine aged heart,
Howe'er he slight thee, thou hast done thy part.
  Oh, barbarous! wouldst thou with a Gothic hand
Pull down the schools—what!—all the schools i' th' land;
Or throw them up to livery-nags and grooms,
Or turn them into shops and auction-rooms?
A captious question, sir, (and yours is one,)
Deserves an answer similar, or none.
Wouldst thou, possessor of a flock, employ
(Apprised that he is such) a careless boy,
And feed him well, and give him handsome pay,
Merely to sleep, and let them run astray?
Survey our schools and colleges, and see
A sight not much unlike my simile.

From education, as the leading cause,
The public character its colour draws;
Thence the prevailing manners take their cast,
Extravagant or sober, loose or chaste.
And though I would not advertise them yet,
Nor write on each—This Building to be Let,
Unless the world were all prepared to embrace
A plan well worthy to supply their place;
Yet, backward as they are, and long have been,
To cultivate and keep the MORALS clean,
(Forgive the crime,) I wish them, I confess,
Or better managed, or encouraged less.

William Cowper – A Short Biography

William Cowper was born 26th November 1731 in Berkhamsted, Hertfordshire, where his father John Cowper was the rector of the Church of St Peter. His mother was Ann née Donne (a relative of the great poet, John Donne). Only Cowper, the eldest child, and his brother John, out of seven children, survived past infancy. Ann died giving birth to John on 7th November 1737. His mother's death when he was only six was deeply traumatising to the young Cowper. Indeed, a half century later it was used as the basis of his poem, 'On the Receipt of My Mother's Picture'. The tragedy did however draw him closer to the rest of her side of the family. He was particularly close with his uncle Robert and his wife Harriot. It was their influence that engendered in him a love of reading, and their literary gifts, John Bunyan's Pilgrim's Progress and John Gay's Fables, opened his eyes to the world of writing.

After moving from school to school for several years he was, in the April of 1742, enrolled into Westminster school, popular at the time amongst prominent Whig supporting families. Cowper made many lifetime friendships at the school as well as a devotion to Latin which he later used in his poetry translations as well as his own verse.

Particularly at Westminster he read and was inspired by Homer's 'The Iliad' and 'The Odyssey'. His later translations of both works were often regarded as seminal.

After leaving Westminster Cowper was articled to Mr Chapman, solicitor, of Ely Place, Holborn, for training in the legal profession. During this period his leisure time was spent at his uncle Robert's home where he fell in love with his cousin, Theodora. However Robert thought that the marriage of persons so closely related was improper and refused the pleas of both nephew and daughter. Cowper took the decision particularly hard.

In 1763 he was offered a Clerkship of Journals in the House of Lords. With the examinations approaching Cowper had a mental breakdown. He tried to commit suicide three times and a period of depression and insanity seemed to settle on him. He was sent to Nathaniel Cotton's asylum at St. Albans for recovery. It was in the aftermath of one suicide attempt that he wrote the poem 'Hatred and vengeance, my eternal portions' (often referred to as 'Sapphics') was written. The end of this unhappy period saw him find refuge in fervent evangelical Christianity, and it was also the inspiration behind his much-loved hymns.

After recovering, he settled at Huntingdon with the retired clergyman Morley Unwin and his wife Mary. Cowper became such good friends with them both that he moved into their house and then with them when they moved to Olney. It was there he met a former captain of a slave ship, now curate, who had now devoted his life to the gospel; John Newton. Shortly afterwards Morley Unwin fell from his horse and died. Cowper continued to live in the Unwin home and became even closer to the widow Mary.

Newton invited Cowper to contribute to a hymnbook that he was compiling. The resulting volume, 'Olney Hymns', although not published until 1779 includes hymns such as 'Praise for the Fountain Opened' and 'Light Shining out of Darkness' which to this day remain some of Cowper's most familiar verses.

However dark forces were about to overwhelm Coper. In 1773, he experienced a devastating attack of insanity, believing that he was eternally condemned to hell, and that God was instructing him to make a sacrifice of his own life. With great care and devotion Mary Unwin nursed him back to health and, after a year, he began to recover.

In 1779, Newton had moved from Olney to London, their 'Olney Hymns' was published and once more Cowper began to write verse. Mary, wanting to keep Cowper's mind occupied, suggested that he write on the subject of 'The Progress of Error'. After writing a satire of this name, he wrote seven others. These poems were collected and printed in 1782 as 'Poems by William Cowper, of the Inner Temple, Esq.'

In 1781 Cowper had the good fortune to meet a sophisticated and charming widow named Lady Austen who inspired a new bout of poetry writing. Cowper himself tells of the genesis of what some have considered his most substantial work, 'The Task', in his "Advertisement" to the original edition of 1785:

...a lady, fond of blank verse, demanded a poem of that kind from the author, and gave him the SOFA for a subject. He obeyed; and, having much leisure, connected another subject with it; and, pursuing the train of thought to which his situation and turn of mind led him, brought forth at length, instead of the trifle which he at first intended, a serious affair—a Volume!

The volume also includes 'The Diverting History of John Gilpin', a notable piece of comic verse and a poem entitled 'Mary'.

Cowper and Mary Unwin moved to Weston Underwood, Buckinghamshire in 1786, having become close to his cousin and Theodora's sister, Lady Harriett Hesketh. He now began his translations from the original Greek into blank verse of Homer's 'The Iliad' and 'The Odyssey'. These new translations, published in 1791, were the most significant English renderings of these epic and classic poems since those of Alexander Pope earlier in the century.

Mary Unwin died in 1796, plunging Cowper into a gloom from which he never fully recovered. He did however continue to revise his Homer for a second edition. Aside from writing the powerful and bleak poem, 'The Castaway', he penned some English translations of Greek verse and translated some of the Fables of John Gay into Latin.

William Cowper was seized with dropsy (an old word for the medical condition edema, an accumulation of fluid in the body leading to swelling) and died on 25th April 1800.

He is buried in the chapel of St Thomas of Canterbury, St Nicholas's Church, East Dereham. A window in Westminster Abbey also honours him.

Cowper was one of the most popular poets of his era and changed the direction of 18th-century nature poetry by writing of everyday life and scenes of the English countryside. He can be seen as a forerunner of Romantic poetry. Coleridge called him the 'the best modern poet', and William Wordsworth was particularly taken by his poem 'Yardley-Oak'. William Wilberforce, the driving force behind the abolition of slavery, referred to Cowper as 'his favourite poet'.

Cowper wrote a number of anti-slavery poems and was asked to write in support of the Abolitionist campaign. His poem 'The Negro's Complaint' (1788) rapidly became famous. He also wrote several other poems on slavery, many of which attacked the idea that slavery made any economic sense.

William Cowper – A Concise Bibliography

Olney Hymns (1779) (in collaboration with John Newton)
Poems by William Cowper (1782)
The Task (1785)
The Diverting History of John Gilpin (1785)
Homer's Iliad (1791) (A translation in blank verse from the Greek)
The Odyssey by Homer (1791) (A translation in blank verse from the Greek)

Made in the USA
Coppell, TX
19 January 2024

27911807R00090